A hospital chaplain writes:

"Dr. Demaray has put togethe inclusion of silence, humor, a. me as an oncology chaplain and pastor. The use of real life stories and biblical material makes the lessons come alive in the reader's spirit."

—B. Dow Cobb, M.Div., B.C.C., Oncology Chaplain,
Joseph Hospital, Lexington, KY and Pastor, Hopewell
Presbyterian Church, Paris, KY

A rehab doctor responds:

"After I read an early version of *Rekindled: Rising from the Ashes of Burnout*, I could only think, 'Where was this book during my intern year?' I saw in this volume so many strategies for fighting my way out of burnout, but I had to figure many of these out on my own."

—Kathleen Davenport-Cobble, M.D.,
2012-13 Fellow at Sports and Spine Hospital for Special
Surgery, New York City

A counseling professor says,

"I wish I had read this book before my own burnout experience and before the many years of counseling with persons experiencing burnout. The reader will want to recommend it to friends, church groups and social service counselors."

—Burrell Dinkins, Th.D., Emeritus Professor of Pastoral
Care and Counseling, Asbury Theological Seminary,
Atlanta, GA

A Hospice director comments:

"Thank you for sharing this insightful and creative book about helping caregivers cope and learn from their stress-related challenges. The life stories, quotes and lessons inspire and lift the reader. This book will serve as a wonderful resource for many people."

—Gail McGillis, Director, Hospice Care Plus, Berea/
Richmond, KY

From a Renovare team member:

"How fortunate we are to have available this up-dated and current work on rekindling our inner lives from Dr. Don, the consummate teacher of truths! With a clear definition of what burnout is, it cancels many misconceptions and puts emphasis on the ways to heal it. The encouragement to live with love, forgiveness and humor is given in just the right doses for a divine cure. The examples from other lives help one relate and soldier on."

—Marti Ensign, speaker and board member of Renovare,
Olympia, WA

A missionary of 31 years responds:

"Everybody interested in personal spiritual formation should read this book! Knowing how to flourish while surviving is much better than suffering burnout and then seeking to rise again. As a person who learned the hard way how to survive, I wholeheartedly recommend reading this book as a daily devotional."

—Martha Kirkpatrick, retired missionary to Central Africa,
Indianapolis, Indiana

The pastor of a thriving town church writes:

"I'm so grateful for this needed and happy reminder that God intends us to run marathons, not just sprints, and that the secret of a well-run race does not depend upon the runner's talent, but on the runner's ability to see the race for what it is."

—Daryl Diddle, Senior Pastor, Free Methodist Church,
Wilmore, KY

A professor of spiritual formation writes as follows:

"Like a drink of cold water renews our strength, this book rekindles our hope. And when we are burned out, there's no greater gift than that. Don Demaray knows how to connect us with God, the source of that hope, and how to offer real-life practices that the Spirit can use to lead us from darkness to light."

—Dr. Steve Harper, Professor Emeritus of Spiritual Formation and
Wesley Studies, Asbury Theological Seminary, Orlando, FL

A city pastor says:

"Don Demaray has done it again! He's placed in the hands of busy, hardworking people a tool that will literally save their lives. He writes with humor and warmth about the wide range of matters that can lead to burnout and provides a path for healing and a return to vitality. Last summer Eugene Peterson's *The Pastor* provided the soul renewal I desperately needed. *Rekindled* is in the same vein; an oasis for souls traveling too fast and fraying at the edges. This is a vitally important book!"

—Dan Johnson, Senior Pastor,
Trinity United Methodist Church, Gainesville, FL

# Rekindled

## *Rising from the*
## *Ashes of Burnout*

Donald E. Demaray

EMETH PRESS
www.emethpress.com

*Rekindled, Rising from the Ashes of Burnout*

Copyright © 2013 Donald E. Demaray
Printed in the United States of America on acid-free paper

Library of Congress Cataloging-in-Publication Data

Demaray, Donald E.
  Rekindled : rising from the ashes of burnout / Donald E. Demaray.
      pages cm
  Includes bibliographical references.
  ISBN 978-1-60947-050-0 (alk. paper)
  1.  Burn out (Psychology) 2.  Change (Psychology) 3.  Spiritual healing. 4. Time management.  I. Title.
  BF481.D4646 2012
  158.7'23--dc23
                      2012044743

Cover graphic is Dove of the Holy Spirit (ca. 1660, alabaster, Throne of St. Peter, St. Peter's Basilica, Vatican) by Gian Lorenzo Bernini (1598–1680). Public Domain.

# DEDICATED TO JAMES

Devoted Christian

Loyal Family Man

Faithful Chaplain

# CONTENTS

# FOREWORD

After I read an early manuscript version of *Rekindled: Rising from the Ashes of Burnout,* I could only think, "Where was this book during my intern year?" I saw in this volume useable strategies for fighting my way out of burnout, but I had to figure many of these out on my own. I had to take time out of work to heal, and when I returned to the workplace I felt saved from the brink, yet not quite healed. A few years must go by before I felt completely myself again. During recovery I noticed improvement each day.

As a doctor, I suffered from burnout during the first year of residency. This year, known in the profession as the *intern year,* is a time of sleep deprivation combined with making daily life-and-death decisions. It is stressful. Many doctors burn out.

The most prominent emotion I feel about this time is embarrassment. Every day I went to work and saw others doing similar jobs without seeming to burn out. Even now I feel somewhat inadequate about what seems like a failure on my part. No one likes to talk about burnout, even to share one-on-one. Though I know most physicians go through something like burnout during their residency years, I somehow think I should have coped, should have figured out a way to survive without the letdown. Nonetheless, I now feel better and more compassionate both with my patients and colleagues because of this trying experience.

Burnout is not something benign, fleeting, or simple. It takes control of one's life, can disable the doctor from caring effectively for patients. Do not misunderstand—I did not make medical errors. My patients, protected and safe under my care, experienced no external damage from my internal wounds. However, I was not the doctor I wanted to be, could be, or am now.

A senior resident, able to recognize my burnout symptoms, deserves a lot of credit. She assured me burnout occurs frequently; in fact, she confessed, she too had gone through the depressive experience. She intervened, guiding me through the healing process. For example, she suggested a much-needed respite. Time off facilitated cure.

The following year I identified an intern with similar symptoms and had the joy of helping her navigate successfully through the storm. Another colleague moved to a different city for medical practice—the new setting played a part in his cure from burnout. From now on, wherever my own workplace, I will stay alert for assisting colleagues who may suffer from burnout.

The most important healing strategies for me included talking with my husband and pacing myself. Other strategies I learned not only from reading but also in professional clinical experience, which proved both humbling and enlightening. For example, I discovered that no one expected me to shoulder burdens I had erroneously placed on myself.

My university is highly active in providing resident doctors opportunities for counseling, stress management, prevention, and treatment. What the university advised and what my husband counseled agreed: recapture perspective, shift from a negative to a positive attitude, and maintain focus.

Pacing is another matter altogether. In residency one has little control over schedule or assignments, yet I learned time-management techniques of my own. When I spoke to authorities about the need for redoing schedule, I stood in actual shock at how I got a revised program. It pays to ask!

Then, I learned to edit out any activity not really necessary. I did not have to attend all recommended conferences—most particularly those unrelated to my specialty. Conferences not attended made possible closing some work days with a little time left over. Also in the course of a day, I could step outside for a breath of fresh air or find a secluded place for the quiet required for recapturing a clear head.

Some of my colleagues, on the other hand, really liked conference opportunities. For them, these opportunities provided a way of getting away from demanding clinical routine and finding renewal. Each doctor must discover what he or she requires for body and soul health.

For me, this *Rekindled* book provides a path not only for recovering from burnout, but also for marching toward a fulfilling and rewarding career. It is a guide for the long run while still addressing short-term needs. Moreover, I sense the timeliness of the book. With the economy in crisis and budgets cut, we are asked to do more with less. God wants the best out of us, and this publication provides ways to liberate us to work at optimum level.

Kathleen L. Davenport, MD
Resident Physician
Physical Medicine and Rehabilitation
University of Washington
Seattle, Washington

(Kathleen is in her last year of residency at the University of Washington. She will start a Sports and Spine Fellowship at the Hospital for Special Surgery in New York City in the coming academic year.)

# ACKNOWLEDGMENTS

This book would not have come to fruition without the probing of my son James, a Hospice chaplain, who wanted a guide for himself and his colleagues to stay well in the midst of daily work with end-of-life people. The strain of ministering to the elderly and dying can "get to you, Dad. You wrote a book on burnout years ago and we need that reprinted." From there I consulted with publisher Larry Wood of Emeth Press. He encouraged me with a contract.

Happy for both the suggestion and encouragement, I discovered that a reprint of the book would not do the job for busy people in our current world. I would need to make changes, not just here and there, but major alterations in research and accessible prose. This project took longer than anticipated and proved a most interesting and satisfying endeavor.

So thanks first to son James and publisher Wood. Further gratitude must go to Sheila Lovell gifted with the *school marm* expertise of a teacher of English grammar and syntax. No two eyes see everything (I repeat that over and over to my writing classes), and sure enough, Sheila saw things—quite a lot in fact—that I overlooked. Thank you, Sheila.

Thank you also to Judy Seitz, Senior Editor, Doctor of Ministry Program, Asbury Theological Seminary. She is a precisionist. Lisa Setters, Research and Library Loan Specialist, Asbury Seminary, tracked down documentation data from time to time. Like Judy, Lisa can pride herself on careful work.

Steve Milans, my faithful computer man, instructs me in the wizardry of electronics. I could not function without his expert and gracious help.

Candace Hardin, one of my former doctoral students—and one of the best—serves as a hospital chaplain in Arkansas. Asked by her hospital administration to help build a wellness program for employees, she tackled current research on health and wholeness, especially burnout. Upon hearing that, I gathered up my courage to ask this very busy professional to read quite a lot of my work and make suggestions. She graciously complied and graced the manuscript with improvements. Thank you, Candace.

At the time of this writing, my granddaughter, Kathleen, is a physician-in-residence at University of Washington. She suffered burnout which turned out to be an overture to helpful discoveries. The University of Washington Medical College, concerned about the welfare of their doctors, maintains an active program designed to assist medical personnel to stay healthy. More, Kathleen went to counseling and learned not only of clues to healing from burnout but also how to stay well. In the light of the university's careful and scientific program, and Kathleen Davenport-Cobble's personal experience, she consented to write the Foreword to this work. I find myself both grateful and proud.

How can I thank the many who talked over coffee, completed my research instrument, and favored me with interviewing time? These courtesies came in the midst of busy ministry in Canada, America, South Africa, and the United Kingdom. Always I found a sympathetic and listening ear, along with comments both revealing and therapeutic. This interchange not only introduced me to the phenomenon we now call burnout but also served as motivation to research and write to help hurting people. Soon I learned that people of all vocations—not only clergy—can suffer this vicious onslaught. That fresh awareness broadened my perspective to see fundamental principles of health and well-being for all burdened laborers, whatever their calling. Perhaps people who relate to the helping professions and ministries—clergy, social workers, teachers, mothers, caregivers—are the most vulnerable. At any rate people of all vocations came into my purview.

Thank you to Baker Book House for permission to redo my earlier work, *Watch Out for Burnout: A Look at Its Signs, Prevention, and Cure* (1983). For the new title, *Rekindled: Rising from the Ashes of Burnout,* I am indebted to Martha Sparks, writer friend. Thank you, Martha.

# INTRODUCTION

"Never look down to test the ground before taking your next step; only he who keeps his eye fixed on the far horizon will find the right road."

(This grand therapeutic comment comes from the late, hard-working Secretary General of the United Nations, Dag Hammarskjold. A committed believer, Swedish-born Dag Hammarskjold knew the power of God and belief).

E. Stanley Jones' mission endeavor in India, with its years of hard work, exhausted his resources despite twelve months of furlough in America. On board ship, returning to India, he conducted a Sunday service only to collapse. Embarrassed, he found himself in the grip of inner torment. How could he continue missionary work? He would soon make the most important discovery of his life.

Back in India his mind recounted over and over his failure. He went to the mountains to recapture his health, but the time apart left him destitute. He admitted to himself, "I am finished and must go back to America."

In his own words, Dr. Jones tells what happened next:

In that dark hour I was in the Central Methodist Church in Lucknow. The Rev. Tamil David was in charge of the evangelistic services. I was at the back of the church kneeling in prayer, not for myself but for others, when God said to me: "Are you yourself ready for the work to which I have called you?" My reply: "No, Lord, I'm done for, I've reached the end of my resources and I can't go on." "If you'll turn that problem over to me and not worry about it, I'll take care of it." My eager reply: "Lord. I close the bargain right here." I rose from my knees knowing I was a well man.

Walking home with a group of missionaries Jones felt he was advancing on air. Possessed of Life with a capital L, Stanley Jones knew joy and peace. He hardly needed sleep and believed he must now give public testimony to the miracle, but his friends cautioned him lest he fall back into burnout. But he knew better, for when he put his full weight down, he felt only solid support underneath. No longer looking downward, he saw the horizon ablaze with glorious possibilities.

Today a plaque hangs in the Lucknow Church: "Near this spot Stanley Jones knelt a physically broken man and arose a physically well man." The tablet, testifies Dr. Jones, communicated what happened only in part, for the total person, not only the physical, came to resurrection.

Body, mind, and spirit experienced renewal. Flooded with energy, he knew no mere moment of good feeling, a passing phenomenon that would leave him destitute of adequacy. "God was not playing hide and seek, coming and going. This was being taken possession of by the Holy Spirit, the 'Spirit of Truth' who should abide forever" (Jones, *A Song of Ascents* ch. 6).

From that point on, through his long life of demanding work, his eyes saw only the horizon. Even in his late years of recovering from a stroke, his spirits still possessed of God's Spirit, he learned to walk again and preached the Life-giving gospel of Jesus Christ.

# PROLOGUE

Persons of all vocations suffer burnout. A study of one seminary's alumni indicates that burnout most often happens five years after graduation. Other research shows American schoolteachers burn out between the fifth and sixth years of service.

Multiple causes account for dropout, but studies indicate that acute fatigue and persistent frustrations are significant dynamics. The following studies revealed early on that burnout is a significant cause of dropout:

> The duration-of-service norm for inner-city social workers and inner-city lawyers turns out to be only two years.

> One American psychiatrist says 50 percent of his clients are missionaries.

> A seasoned missionary observes that the typical overseas worker lasts five to six years.

> A large denomination reported, some years ago, clergy losses at 1,000 per annum. That figure has jumped to the current rate of 1200 to 1500 a month. This astonishing but accurate data boggles the mind (see Demaray and Pickerill, *A Robust Ministry*).

Homemakers go through burnout, too. Marriages often run into difficulty after five years. Boredom and depression can threaten families.

How do we cope with this threat called burnout?

*Recognizing signals helps. Signs of oncoming burnout, documented by experienced counselors, include diminution of enthusiasm, gray feelings, negativity, cynicism, withdrawal, lowering of competence, absenteeism, sluggish thinking, anger, and stress. As distress deepens, disgust, paralysis, radical isolation, full-scale depression, and inability to plan and work can rear their ugly heads.

*Dealing with this multifaceted phenomenon also calls for unloading verbally. One's spouse may help. We human beings sometimes have a hard time coming to grips with what bugs us. Part of the reason lodges in the subconscious. While the conscious mind involves itself in the immediate enterprises of everyday work and life, the subliminal mind packs away the negatives, including trivialities that stack up in hidden recesses. A good spouse often knows how to pull these secrets from the closet of our brain and bring positive, healing perspective to his or her mate.

*Sometimes a confidant will sort out the frustration points. Often a person important to us, one we see as an authority figure, comes to our rescue. A professional therapist may ask just the right questions and pinpoint issues. In addition, some find journaling useful; journaling often results in self-help, which results from the "aha" moments of insight.

Here's one not-to-be-forgotten principle: Listeners to hurting people must hear with love and empathy; judging only exacerbates hurt and pain, for already negatives like guilt and shame haunt the struggling person. Mother Teresa rightly observes that to judge is to rob one of the ability to love. Loving listening often results in the magic of therapy.

*Once in a while acute distress requires a job change, though finding a new job may present a formidable challenge. When possible, fresh employment can initiate clarity of vision. But running away from crisis can create bigger problems; facing crisis often flowers into enlarged freedom, creativity, and productivity.

*Nor must we forget in-depth prayer, an enterprise all of us learn more and more about from crisis to crisis. The disciples' plea to our Lord, "Teach us to pray" (Luke 11), can lead to enormously therapeutic results. A study of the first 13 verses of Luke 11 may result in very welcome coping grace. Moreover, the Spirit sometimes speaks so quietly that only silence, deep interior stillness, opens our ears to listen and act. But merely to escape taxing responsibility by isolation from people and challenges will not work. Solitude—the quiet heart and mind in the Presence of God's Spirit—brings answers and the fulfillment that spells peace.

*Do prioritize the calendar for unhurried time with family and friends, full-scale recreation, also adequate sleep and nutrition. Creating a slower lifestyle, engaging in hobbies, and developing a systematic exercise program may function as effective instruments of healing.

*Humor proves itself a genuine remedy and preventative. John Milton, in his *L'Allegro,* intuited the therapeutic power of laughter:

> Sport that wrinkled care derides,
> And laughter holding both his sides,
> Come, and trip it as ye go
> On the light fantastic toe.

\*\*\*                          \*\*\*                          \*\*\*

Whatever the prescription, we aim to find Edwin Markham's "place of central calm" at the "heart of the cyclone tearing the sky." *To help people find that central calm— deep abiding peace—is the target of this book.*

# A NOTE TO THE READER

In this book, help comes packaged in digestible units. Single meditation readings indicate causes and suggest cures; these I have designated by the medical sign for prescription—*Rx* followed by *info-med* for *information* and *meditation*.

Thirteen crucial areas of cause and cure provide the book's framework. In each of the thirteen divisions you will find seven sections. You may want to use this little volume over a quarter of a year for small group interaction (13 sections in 13 weeks, each week divided into 7 days) or for private reading and processing.

Best of all, the material opens one to the dynamically fresh work of the Holy Spirit, Author of health and well-being.

# WEEK 1:

# REKINDLED: FACING BURNOUT

Whether you are involved in someone else's Burn-Out or your own, take heart. In every fire, there are glowing embers. You can use them to rekindle the spark.

—Herbert J. Freudenberger
*Burn-Out: The High Cost of Achievement*

## *Day 1*

## *WHAT IS BURNOUT?*

*Rx info-med*

Psychiatrist Herbert J. Freudenberger invented the term *burnout* to describe his own experience. Working in the free clinic movement of the 1960s, he grew severely disappointed. For years he operated a clinic but could see little result. He saw countless persons daily in spite of his physical exhaustion and emotional drain and never got to bed before one or two in the morning.

Dr. Freudenberger's regular practice kept him busy from 8 a.m. to 6 p.m. After that he hurried to the downtown clinic that stayed open to 11 o'clock. In the wee hours of the morning, he returned home. Fatigue pushed him harder; his wife tried to caution him, but he could only respond with irritation. After all, these patients needed help, and he would try with all his might.

Now his wife, concerned about Herbert's wan look and lingering sinus infection, insisted on a Christmas vacation with family. She made reservations for air travel and accommodation. He dropped into bed at 2 a.m., fully expecting to pack for the vacation in the morning. But morning came only to find him incapacitated; he slept nonstop for two days. On the third day, though unable to get out of bed, he could at least reflect on what happened. He was working twenty hours a day, driving himself on a "madman course" he could not stop. Clearly, something had gone terribly wrong.

Why was he cheating himself and his family of time and vacation? Why was he living such an unreasonable life? He must discover the dynamics of this strange behavior.

The vacation period gave him time to talk into a tape recorder. The day after the first recording, his own voice shocked him—a terrible and revealing mix of anger, irritation, depression, and arrogance.

Continuing for several days talking into the recorder, he made further discoveries. "The tapes gave me important insights into myself," he said, and he wrote an article that "served as a catharsis" (p. xx). Now he knew he must prioritize himself, putting his life into balance in terms of family, health, patients, and the need to make a living.

The forces that drove him to overdo included the number of homeless, hurting children; an inadequate physical plant; too few trained helpers; an uncaring community; plus, of course, his regular daytime practice. But he realized another driving force—his childhood in Nazi Germany. This experience gave him an especially sensitive heart for homeless kids, for he had seen children abandoned, their parents carted off to concentration camps and even killed in Hitler's holocaust.

All the above factors coming together caused Dr. Freudenberger's collapse, which he called *burnout*. Thus the name, now familiar to the world, came to birth. However, with that breakthrough in identification, he also sensed hope. Burnout signals not despair but hope, he said, for with fresh realizations, one can say *stop, look, listen!* and heal.

Dr. Freudenberger fought burnout creatively. He wrote on burnout, describing causes and cures. He spent more time with his family, taking vacations instead of trying to use every spare hour to cure the ills of his patients. He revamped his work schedule for a fresh lease on his life and his profession. He would not entertain defeat. He found a way out.

\*\*\*            \*\*\*                 \*\*\*

*Not despair but hope*—that awareness translates negative thinking and depression into a positive attitude and outlook. Cynicism, gossip, anger, rigidity, pessimism, and an unwillingness to listen now submit to flexibility, empathy, and a confident outlook. Overintensity in goal

achievement—push, push, push—unbendingly high expectations, really a kind of perfectionism, now begins to
reverse itself into normalcy, into the relaxed posture, the
peace, which the Creator intended.

### Rekindled? Yes!

\*\*\*                    \*\*\*                    \*\*\*

Whatever our vocation, burnout can threaten us. The pastor holds high moral ideals for his young people but sees
them caught in the clutches of peer pressure and sin; the
doctor cannot alleviate all the suffering of her patients;
the social worker finally gets money to help a family in
poverty only to have it refused by the very people who
need it. We must face reality—some things we leave in
God's hands. We cannot do the impossible.

Yet we try, but idealism yields to life's brutalities. How
does one live with that? One can clam up and withdraw,
protecting the self momentarily from hurt. One can fade
away from full participation, thus depriving oneself of
liberated joy. One can become a battering ram, persisting
while suffering more wounds and damaging others.

# Day 2
## THE SYMPTOMS OF BURNOUT

*Rx info-med*

The hallmarks of burnout include boredom, frustration, domestic problems, hopelessness, rejection, paranoia, pessimism, stress, meaninglessness, enervation, and irritability. All of us have some of these feelings some of the time, especially after heavy-duty work such as meeting a major deadline, moving from one community to another, or arranging a public event. A good day or two off, sometimes a week, usually takes care of the exhaustion and we're ready for life again.

But chronic weariness can sneak up on us. Fatigue sets in. We find chatter annoying; we go in circles with little to show for effort invested; we begin to turn sour on life, fight inner heaviness, snap at family and friends, isolate ourselves from routine social contacts, feel terribly harried, and let important dates and facts skip from memory. We may even show psychosomatic distress—pain in the stomach, headaches, back and perhaps joint pain, or persistent respiratory ailments and infection—just to name a few diseases that can attack us.

When we cannot laugh, especially at ourselves, that's a pretty good sign something has gone wrong. Some also find that they cannot cry.

Teachers who invest in their students, only to suffer rejection, may suffer burnout. Young professionals who graduate from university under the illusion they can *handle everything* need warning flags waving in full view. The flags tell us the real world doesn't yield to quick and competent answers. When standards elude and goals evade us, we come face-to-face with the disconnect between our ideals and things as they are. When we see little success, life deals its blows.

The varying names we give burnout in our contemporary society help us isolate and define symptoms. One of my graduate students, Candace Hardin, a hospital chaplain and researcher, sent me this list of synonyms for burnout:

Compassion Fatigue
Provider Fatigue
Empathy Fatigue
Emotional/Spiritual Traumatization
Vicarious Traumatization
Empathic Engagement Fatigue
Cost of Caring
Spiritual/Emotional Distress
Wounded-by-the-Work Syndrome
Caregiver Fatigue/Distress
Wear-and-Tear Syndrome
Emotional Over-Extension

This list, incomplete to be sure, suggests identifying factors and causes of burnout. Note, for example, how often the term fatigue occurs. Later we will come to grips with fatigue and address the commonly occurring Compassion Fatigue.

If we can isolate the marks and causes of burnout, we can also find cures. The people who really take a day or two off after a big event know part of the secret. So do those who eat good food, sleep well, talk with God, and dialog with their spouse and friends. Those who slow down and define success realistically, yet without compromise, have found a cure.

### *Rekindled? Yes!*

# Day 3
# WHY ME?

### *Rx info-med*

Why me? Over-commitment.

Church and school teach us to give ourselves in total commitment to God and our work, but that grand truth requires perspective for living it out with freedom and liberated enthusiasm. Jesus never lost sleep because He couldn't preach outside the Palestinian strip; He called Paul and his friends to do that. Jesus did not win all the people; His own brothers refused to believe in Him until after the resurrection. Jesus did not frustrate Himself about the incongruities of life; He left family, friends and situations in the hands of the sovereign God.

Jesus ministered within the framework of His own style. He never allowed people to dictate how He went about His mission–He stayed true to Himself. He did not allow persons to define commitment for Him–He and His Father wrote the definition.

How do you define total commitment? Society often describes it as overachieving. Our culture (sometimes even our Christian culture) creates compulsive persons with a perfectionist streak, people who suffer from a terrible *mustness* to succeed and change the world.

Have we forgotten that only God knows how to change the world? Recognize Him as omniscient, all-knowing. Let Him determine your own personal role in world change. Refuse to allow an outsized drive to determine your place in society. What He assigns, do in His strength. Sincere plodders often achieve more in a lifetime than fiery men and women who wear out prematurely. Think of the tortoise and the hare.

Had the Old Testament prophet, Elijah, lived in contemporary America, he might have been a coronary Type A person. Medical researchers define Type A behavior as a complex of factors observed in people aggressively involved in a chronic and incessant fight to achieve much more in much less time, and the fight results in unreasonable energy cost. Dollars, numbers of people and buildings, deadlines—signs of personal achievement and success—can define unrealistic commitment. Highly motivated women and men can fall into this trap (for more, GOOGLE Type A Behavior).

This lifestyle produces chronic stress, which may trigger high blood pressure, unwanted cholesterol, heart attacks, even diabetes. *Because Type A behavior may be learned, we can unlearn, or at least modify, it—that's the good news.*

The Old Testament prophet, Elijah, had to unlearn stressful living. He unlearned it the hard way. The Bible pictures him as a speed runner, hard-hitting preacher, inspired faith-builder, rugged outdoorsman, and triumphant challenger. Over-intense and overachieving, he paid the price, as we shall see. We shall also notice how he found renewal, fresh meaning in life, and a recovered sense of God's presence.

### *Rekindled? Yes!*

# Day 4
# ELIJAH'S PEAK EXPERIENCE

*Rx info-med*

D. B. Kehl, in an article for *Christianity Today*, aptly entitled "Burnout: The Risk of Reaching Too High," observes that burnout may come after peak experiences such as Elijah's Mt. Carmel victory.

Imagine the prophet's emotional investment with half a thousand pagan prophets pitted against him—the mammoth test of faith, the dynamic flow of events, the intense dialog, and the climax of fire falling and consuming the sacrifice, wood, stone, and water. This enormously demanding experience would naturally take its emotional and spiritual toll, even from one with a strong constitution.

Great crises drain human beings. Elijah's letdown ranged from emotional fatigue to lethargy and melancholia (1 Kings 19).

Some published authors testify that their great letdowns follow the completion of writing projects. Internal conflicts rage while the mind rushes into dark and discolored alleyways: *Why didn't I write a better historical novel? Surely this short story will give rise to reader rejection. The research on this article will prove inadequate.*

Writers, like all artists, must wait for their emotions to return to normal. They reject the raging inner conflict by letting time do its magic. They rest from the intense enthusiasm required to bring a fresh creation to completion. *Mission accomplished* means glands no longer provide energy to match the challenge; the search for stimuli to generate productivity comes to a standstill. One's perspective alters as reentry takes place.

Wise achievers (1) expect letdown and plan for it; (2) keep their cool during and immediately after reentry; and (3) refurbish body, mind, and spirit by relaxation, diversion and worship.

**Rekindled? Yes!**

# Day 5
## HANDLING REJECTION

### *Rx info-med*

Jezebel informed Elijah she would wipe him out within twenty-four hours. Most of us will not experience rejection in such radical form, but the prophet did and the result was a chain of negative thoughts that made him feel worthless.

Rejection sets up an inner dialog that spells self-doubt. We fear that people have only tolerated us, that in reality we just haven't *made it*. This persistent negative thinking leads to depression.

No wonder Elijah withdrew to the wilderness. Such behavior is both wise and symptomatic, yet we admire Elijah who, prior to isolation, played the game with all his might. Some people never get on life's stage because they don't want to risk themselves.

Nathaniel Hawthorne dreamed of writing a play but it never materialized. The outline, discovered in the papers he left, shows clearly the possibilities of the plot. The drama's development might have proved mysterious and fascinating because the chief character never once appears; he speaks and acts from the shadows. Perhaps Hawthorne was afraid to risk play writing.

Elijah did not do his thing in a corner, hidden and protected from the possibilities of rejection. He got out there on the stage and played his part, though his critics shot at him. And he won!

How do we handle rejection before it draws us into the abyss of depression? First, face your anger. Rejection's hurt is the obverse side of anger, and anger has power to defeat and depress us. Second, having faced rejection, deal with your unreleased emotions by playing a fast game of raquetball, jogging, chopping and hauling wood, or throwing yourself into just about any wholesome, vigorous activity. Aim to use up the adrenalin. Third, develop the defense of humor. Virtually every rejection has its funny side, and wit has a way of dissolving negative impact. Fourth, always pray for grace to love the one who offends you.

**Rekindled? Yes!**

# Day 6

## ELIJAH RECOVERS FROM DEPRESSION

### *Rx info-med*

Elijah's rejection and resulting anger dissolved into depression. Fear gripped him; isolation came next, suicidal thoughts tormented him; terrible solitude bore in upon him. First Kings 19 carries not only the story of Elijah's black emotions but also the parallel account of God's therapy. Elijah calls on God with agonizing feelings: "It is enough; now, Lord, take away my life; for I am no better than my fathers." Listen to Eugene Peterson's account of Elijah's misery:

> When Elijah saw how things were, he ran for dear life to Beersheba, far in the south of Judah. He left his young servant there and then went on into the desert another day's journey. He came to a lone broom bush and collapsed in its shade, wanting in the worst way to be done with it all–to just die: "Enough of this, GOD! Take my life–I'm ready to join my ancestors in the grave!" Exhausted, he fell asleep under the lone broom bush (1 Kings 19:3-4, *The Message*).

Elijah awakened from the escape of sleep at the touch of an angel: "Arise and eat." After eating and drinking, he fell asleep again. The angel awakened him a second time to eat and drink.

During the next forty days, Elijah traveled to Horeb where he took lodging in a cave, a fitting spot for his darkened spirit. God spoke, "What are you doing here,

Elijah?" Elijah's answer betrays his bitterness, egotism, and paranoia: *People do not appreciate me.*

The Lord tried more radical therapy. Summoning Elijah to His presence on Mount Horeb, God sent a great and terrible wind that split rocks open, "but the Lord was not in the wind." Then came a powerful earthquake, "but the Lord was not in the earthquake." Next came a searing fire, "but the Lord was not in the fire" (1 Kings19:11-12).

Peterson's interpretation of this sequence puts it in bold relief:

> A hurricane wind ripped through the mountains and shat-tered the rocks before GOD, but GOD wasn't to be found in the wind; after the wind an earthquake, but GOD wasn't in the earthquake; and after the earthquake fire, but GOD wasn't in the fire; and after the fire a gentle and quiet whis-per (vv. 11-12).

God's fourth communication, "a still small voice," pene-trated Elijah's self-absorbed mind. At first the message proved too painful, and the prophet returned to his cave. "What are you doing here, Elijah?" Bitterness, egocen-tricity, and paranoia answered, *Nobody's good but me, and people want to kill me.*

God knew how to deal with this depressed prophet.

> When Elijah heard the quiet voice, he muffled his face with his great cloak, went to the mouth of the cave, and stood there. A quiet voice asked, "So Elijah, now tell me, what are you doing here?" Elijah said it again, "I've been working my heart out for GOD, the GOD-of-the-Angel-Armies, but the people of Israel have abandoned your covenant, destroyed your places of worship, and murdered your prophets. I'm the

only one left, and now they're trying to kill me" (*The Message*, vv. 13-14).

With this comment the Lord brought therapy to its climax: "Go and do…." Elijah's assignment was the anointing of two kings and the ordination of a young prophet.

*The Message* puts the final piece of the therapy into perspective:

> Elijah went straight out and found Elisha son of Shaphat in a field where there were twelve pairs of yoked oxen at work plowing; Elisha was in charge of the twelfth pair; Elijah went up to him and threw his cloak over him.

> Elisha deserted the oxen, ran after Elijah, and said, "Please! Let me kiss my father and mother good-bye—then I'll follow you."

> "Go ahead," said Elijah, "but, mind you, don't forget what I've just done to you" (vv. 19-20).

Therapy came in God's presence, loving patience, and purposeful assignments. Elijah's sense of personal worth was restored.

### *Rekindled? Yes!*

# Day 7

## FACE FATIGUE AND

## RECEIVE HEALING

### *Rx info-med*

Before God's interventional therapy, Elijah does not appear to have come to grips with his fatigue. He tried several ways to avoid facing his exhaustion. Escape is one; over-activity is another. One avoidance technique says, "Resign everything." Elijah dropped work and turned his back on relationships, even left his servant. The other extreme announces, "Drown weariness in busyness."

To get away is good and to exercise certainly has its benefits, but is mile after mile of labor-intensive hikes in the wilderness and desert really desirable? Both ends of the continuum signal danger.

A young husband walking away from his lovely wife and children comments, "I feel trapped." Close examination reveals an overcrowded schedule. He had achieved success professionally and personally. Fatigue set in long before the surprise exit. He overextended himself until something had to go—in this case, wife and family.

The therapeutic dialog between Elijah and God eventuated in clarity of thought and rational action. The young husband and father should have talked with God and family. Unvented interpersonal tensions create a formula for explosion. Talk provides catharsis; dialog opens windows on fresh awareness, furnishing hope and bringing new possibilities into view.

Standing up to one's fatigue is neither antisocial isolation nor inordinate involvement but the anteroom to establishing sound priorities. This happy equilibrium comes with liberated exploration filled with love and imagination, the very context in which God works.

### Rekindled? Yes!

\*\*\*　　　\*\*\*　　　\*\*\*

Today we talk about Compassion Fatigue, a real threat. Liz Garrison, a young Salvation Army social worker, was excited to begin her new job. Involved in frontline ministry, she would assist helpless people! She dreamed of social change and loved each day, no matter how heavy the work load.

Then she began to notice the diminution of enthusiasm in her colleagues. Liz sensed the stress and demands of serving as a social change person. Strange thoughts and behaviors seemed to arise from nowhere, unless indeed they issued from trying to help traumatized, hurting people. After awhile empathy ran out, and energy leaked away like water from a cracked bucket: "My colleagues and I had to learn to be intentional about how we gave to others in order to sustain ourselves over the long-term," Liz said.

Liz discovered compassion fatigue commonly hits social servants. Hearing heart-rending stories over and over depletes emotional resources and deflates enthusiasm. Psychosomatic symptoms can emerge; the threat of defeat may haunt one; feelings that I-am-responsible-for-this-mess can insert themselves; eventually the helplessness that gives rise to cynicism can demolish one's effectiveness—all these nasty negatives can knock at one's door. Liz Garrison knew full well that any caregiver, not only people in social service, may suffer these symptoms of compassion fatigue.

So what clue does Liz give us for refreshment of spirit?

> In the end, I'm involved in ministry because I believe that God works in the world. And so, to reduce the impact of compassion fatigue in my life, I need to remember that God works in many ways, not just through me and what I do.

Wise! None of us can do God's work without His enablement (Hosking, 16).

Julia Hosking adds wisdom to Liz Garrison's sound comment when she lists six ways to alleviate compassion fatigue:

**\*Observe the Sabbath.** Proper rest is crucial for caregivers dealing with high stress situations. [Pastors, too, and other Sunday laborers must find a Sabbath, a day off to enjoy God's world and give special attention to Him.]

**\*Do A Self-Assessment.** Are there things that can be delegated to others? Can you change anything about your schedule? Are you taking enough time to recharge?

**\*Be Self-Aware.** Know what your *normal* is.

**\*Rebalance Your Caseload.** Do certain clients deplete you? Spread them out across the day or week; share them with co-workers.

**\*Be Careful What You Watch**. The media sensationalizes trauma which can trigger emotional responses.

**\*Engage in Professional Development.** Additional training can help you gain perspective.

*Rekindled? Yes!*

\*\*\*                    \*\*\*                    \*\*\*

## WEEK'S SUMMARY POINT OF HOPE AND HEALING

**God's Spirit rekindles burning embers into life-giving flame.**

# WEEK 2

# REKINDLED: GOD'S HEALING

I believe He [Jesus] was demonstrating that if we can
find what wholeness or salvation is all about, healing
and physical well-being will be a by-product.

—Bruce Larson

*There's a Lot More to Health than Not Being Sick*

# Day 1

# OUR CENTER AND SOURCE OF HEALING

### Rx info-med

Swiss psychiatrist Carl Jung observed in his patients that religious people get well faster, while sick people without faith tend to stay unhealthy. Through the many years since Jung, research on the relation of faith to healing goes on pretty much nonstop. A recent example appears in the *Lexington Herald-Leader* for August 20, 2011 (B 6). This is the bottom line: Faith relates to healing; belief serves as a strong partner in therapy. Some doctors pray with their patients.

Christians spell out this law of healing in more specific terms than Jung and other like-minded psychiatrists and theorists. Gospel-believing psychotherapists refer specifically to the Christian God. Push the true God out of the center, they affirm, and confusion infiltrates the mind. Hearts made for God suffer restlessness without Him. The inner vacuum tailored for God Himself balks at substitutes. Surrender to the Almighty and acknowledgment of Him as crowned King of our world, brings peace. This peace that comes with bottom-line spiritual adjustment is the reverse of the maladjustment that issues in burnout.

Peace (*shalom*) really means wholeness or well-being and relates to the entirety of life. Some Jews name their children *Shalom*, even businesses. A good Jew, after an especially fine meal, may say *shalom*. That great word embraces the grand spectrum of wholesome living. When one lives in harmony with the Creator, the peace that passes all understanding follows. Jesus, the Prince of *shalom* (health and wholeness), came to demonstrate this principle.

### *Rekindled? Yes!*

# Day 2
## HEALING IN THE RAT RACE?

### *Rx info-med*

The electronics revolution stands as a metaphor of the rat race. In the 1980s Morris Maddocks wrote,

> Whereas there were 10 components per silicon chip in 1960, increasing to several hundred by 1970, by 1976 there were 10,000 and a year later over 30,000. Very large-scale integration (VLSI) will bring the production of microcircuits to an equivalent of 100,000 on a chip, which is less than the size of your fingernail, by 1981, and one million components on a quarter-inch square chip are forecast for the mid 1980s. The advent of the microprocessor … now means that a wide range of … skills can be extended or even displaced.

Now we have the iPhone, Twitter, Facebook, Google, blogs, and more. Who knows what else will come? A new electronics nomenclature has invaded our dictionaries, summed up in the term *artificial intelligence*. Some now believe the future of war resides not so much with boots on the ground as invasion of computer systems with debilitating viruses.

We gulp breathlessly at fast-paced developments (except some like Gen-Xers here and there who seem to love fast-paced electronics and disdain anything slow). Our world expands and compresses at the same time. Contemporary satellite communications make available cross-continental phone calls, radio, and television. We board an airplane and in a few hours land in London or

Johannesburg. We travel fast in word, thought, and person, in other words fast verbally, physically, and, yes, viscerally. The whirl of activities leaves us feeling inadequate because we cannot keep up with it all. No wonder we rob our souls of nutrients by mad activism.

Some in our time want to cry, O Lord, why Silicon Valley? Why must we live in a micro- and macro-electronics age? Can we find no relief, no release, from the burned-out feeling that comes with the constant bombardment of stimuli?

Some get by with only mild reactions—the occasional headache, an elevation in blood pressure, a bit of stomach disorder. Many make the adjustments to fast-paced living and new computer programs. Others do not survive so well. But there is a way to find relief.

### Rekindled? Yes!

# Day 3

# THE EUGENE PETERSON STORY

***Rx info-med***

Eugene Peterson, who produced *The Message*, founded a church in Maryland. He tells the story in *The Pastor: A Memoir*. After three years of intensive work, he delighted in seeing a church building go up. Christ the King Church members, having worshipped three years in the basement of the Peterson home, now saw the bricks-and-mortar result of hard work and a magnificent interior, the fruit of creative input. Dozens of church members took pride, along with Pastor Peterson, in the grand accomplishment, a satisfying piece of architecture, the center of Sunday worship.

Then came a slump in the spirit of both parishioners and pastor. Great projects create energy. Finished projects call for rest from arduous labor. This lesson Eugene learned by experience. He calls the next six years his "Badland Years," a figure of speech he gets out of his family's annual drive from Maryland to Montana. On the way the Petersons traveled through the national park called the Badlands. To motor through the Badlands in the family car did not pose much of a challenge—just drive on. Back at the Maryland church, he could find little enthusiasm, not only in himself but also in his parishioners, for "driving on." Didn't his people want to bring others to Christ? Did fishing on Sunday really seem more important than weekly worship? Especially in a new and beautiful sanctuary?

Eugene, little by little, recovered from the Badlands (not quite burnout, call it "brown-out"). He and his wife made Monday a Sabbath—parish work halted with picnic lunch, hiking, relishing God's out-of-doors. That helped.

He also made more time for family life, for writing, and going about his pastoral duties with divine leisure, not hurried, harried attempts. A parish paper now informed the people of his through-the-week activities, helping them identify with the work of God in their community and making them aware that their pastor worked through the week, not just on Sundays.

He met a nun, Sister Genevieve, from whom he learned something new about God's power and role in an evil world. The result was a deepening understanding of life in the Spirit, which brought a certain measure of renewal. Spiritual renewal always issues in fresh enthusiasm.

Perhaps the chief instrument of new energy came from the yearly trips to Eugene's boyhood home in Montana. Visiting the place of his roots—recalling the people who formed him, going to the spots evocative of happy boyhood moments—that whole remembering enterprise strengthened him to carry on year by year in Maryland.

Pastor Peterson and his wife, Janet, waited patiently through the six "Badland" years. In the midst of frustration, sometimes agony, they refused to give up. Hanging in there until rest comes, along with deepened insight into the workings of God, never comes easily. Evidently God looks kindly on persistence. In fact, Eugene and his wife, Jan, did not leave their parish until God called them to other work—the *until* lasted a total of twenty-nine years.

Moreover, Eugene and Jan refused to submit to the temptation to escape. Running away from challenge spoils both opportunity and servant. Dietrich Bonhoeffer understood the rewards of staying. He prayed,

> We can of course shake off the burden which is laid upon us, but only find that we have a still heavier burden to carry—a yoke of our own choosing, the yoke of our self. But Jesus invites all who travail and are heavy laden to throw off their own yoke and take his yoke upon them—and his yoke is easy, and his burden is light. The yoke and burden of Christ are his cross (*VERSE and VOICE* for 20 July 2011).

Staying, not running, brought the Petersons the peace of God, *shalom.*

### Rekindled? Yes!

# Day 4

# THE RENEWING POWER OF CONFESSION, FORGIVENESS, AND THE HOLY SPIRIT

### Rx info-med

When we allow God-substitutes into our lives (how subtly that happens!), we have the powerful therapeutic resource of confession. With real confession comes assurance of sins forgiven and the consequent renewal of the Spirit. St. Jerome, writing in the fourth century from his own ecclesiastical setting, told of the renewal of confession. Pastors lay their hands on confessing sinners, St. Jerome observed, and ask for and receive the return of the Holy Spirit.

Healing takes place when imbedded sins come to the surface to be cleansed away. Healing prayers can facilitate getting at those sins. The penitent sufferer finds immense release. Reconciliation with God and self is powerful therapy. Prescription drugs may gloss over causes, not getting at the root of the problem. Courageously face the dynamics of your burned-out feelings. Hidden sin may be the culprit. And know too that depression and anxiety may require medicine to provide clarity of mind to address spiritual and moral issues.

We can experience daily renewing of the Spirit by sincere prayers. Praying the Lord's Prayer, for example, has great potential for spiritual rejuvenation. St. Augustine saw the daily praying of the Lord's Prayer as "a daily baptism." And Jesus made ever so clear that the healing of the mind, indeed the whole person, finds repose in forgiveness.

### *Rekindled? Yes!*

# Day 5
# ANSWERS TO PAIN

### *Rx info-med*

Pain expresses itself physically, mentally, socially, and spiritually. Some types of cancer inflict little or no physical pain, but the mental agony can be overwhelming. In terminal disease, the sense of isolation defines a real dimension of the pain. People shun the presence of disease and death. Subliminally we say to ourselves, "Some day I will die and could wrestle with pain before death—such as dementia or other causes of dreadful loneliness." Something of that awful sense of desolation can come over one in burnout.

Burnout pain, while in its grip, can seem endless. We cry, "Will I ever recover?"

What answers bring relief?

*Blessed is the family that furnishes a support system, complete with strengthening nourishment. Recall C. S. Lewis absorbing the pain of his wife, Joy, as she lay on a bed of agony due to cancer. Put alongside that picture the passage in the New Testament about "filling up what is lacking in Christ's afflictions" (Col. 1:24, ESV). A friend sees this verse as someone picking up a suitcase filled with suffering and carrying it for the sufferer.

*A godly confidant, one willing to listen, may volunteer "to carry your suitcase." Sensitive listeners permit people to say whatever burdens them. They also let verbalized thoughts come out at their own rate. To force insight wreaks havoc. The Holy Spirit, the ultimate Therapist, inspires genuine awareness on the part of both listener and sufferer. Therapy materializes in the established trust of sharer, listening friend and Holy Spirit.

*Ask for the laying on of hands, as the Scripture instructs (Jas. 5:14). Invite the elders of your local church, trusted lay leaders and caregivers, to join in a service of healing. Prepare yourself by asking God to clear away obstructions to the flow of His divine medicine. You may want to take Holy Communion, with its divine and fresh cleansing, as part of the preparation. Pain often goes away after healing prayers; at other times intercession acts like a seed planted to spring up later, in God's own time.

*Ask your prayer group to sustain you in intercession. An intimate group of believers who talk comfortably about spiritual concerns is the free-flowing vehicle of enormous spiritual power. Take advantage of this potential for the release of pain.

Expect relief from whatever symptoms accompany your burnout pain: depression, oppression, inhibitions, physical fatigue, emotional exhaustion, interpersonal conflicts, whatever.

### Rekindled? Yes!

# Day 6
# HEALERS

### *Rx info-med*

God graces some people with gifts of healing. What characterizes them?

**Availability.** With never-in-a-hurry lifestyle, these special people freely allow God's Spirit to work when and where and how He wills. They let you know by attitude and body language that they welcome hurting people. They sense that God works through people attuned to His Spirit.

**Listening.** Such people hear with ears, mind, and heart. They sense something of the impact of one's pain. They also listen with intuition to fill in the unspoken gaps.

**Vulnerability.** God opened Himself to the cross through Christ. Therapy comes when available listeners risk themselves. Open healers are those who invite anything, who are unafraid and nonthreatened. This posture is contagious, moving from the listening healer to the hurting sharer, thus opening the door to deep, empathetic therapy.

**Surrender.** God's basic spiritual law is surrender. To pretend we can solve deep problems is sheer folly and ultimately unworkable. The character of today's complex concerns overwhelms our unaided abilities. The wise listener-healer knows that when one focuses on personal problems too long, the problem becomes center stage, hiding therapeutic possibilities.

**Intercession.** Jesus intercedes for us. Prayer in the listening-healing context, marked by the presence of Jesus, gives assurance from the only real source of assurance. Praise, joy, anticipation, and total trust characterize effective intercession. Counselor and counselee sense God alive in the power of the resurrected Lord.

**Follow-Up Caring.** Empathetic nurturers concern themselves not only with initial healing but also with convalescence. Like physical recovery, recuperation often takes time and patience. For the emotionally healed, an early step in establishing spiritual health lies in worship. Scripture, praise, song, and sermon communicate powerful stabilizing forces. Faith deepens and becomes an anchor of the soul.

*Koinonia. Koinonia* is fellowship, that sense of warm, caring community, which goes a long way toward healing and stabilizing. Dr. and Mrs. Michael Daves opened their home and dinner table to Kathleen and me after an all-night flight many years ago. The warmth, openness, laughter and joy that permeated the atmosphere of their English home rested us: "Do return. We covet the chance to get better acquainted." Nothing put on, their excited sincerity let us know of their genuine hospitality. We left saying, "The Daves create a model Christian home." God's Spirit gives birth to the flow of soul, which is community, a powerful healing context.

One's church family opens the door to healing. Pastor and people who provide a listening ear help the hurting process their soul sickness. Just now as I write, my wife suffers dementia. She has lost contact with reality, though some capacity for conversation remains. I went to church yesterday with a heavy heart, not knowing the next step for my wife of 63 years. Jerri, the empathetic greeter, shuttled me into the pastor's office. Between services he had time to listen. And listen he did—to my weeping heart. He prayed for Kathleen appropriately in the public pastoral prayer. He did the same in the evening service. Quite naturally, the church members shared their concerns about Kathleen with me at the close of the services. What an uplift! With a church family like this, I have permission to process my grief. (Subsequently the neurologist gave Kathleen medicine and that, with much prayer, has brought her back to reality. While she still forgets, she shows much progress and I am very grateful.)

God puts His children in contact with caring, healing, nurturing people. Welcome the *koinonia*, the community of sharing, He provides.

**Rekindled? Yes!**

# Day 7

# THE THERAPEUTIC POWER OF HOPE

*Rx info-med*

Love brings hope and hope, in turn, initiates healing. Re-searchers know that an orphan baby will decline physi-cally without a mother's love. Sensitive medical people prescribe rocking, holding, even bundling the baby. The medical chart then diagrams medical improvement. (For an interesting commentary on love and infants, see Jones, *Word Become Flesh,* 90.) Clearly love creates a sense of wholesome, excited anticipation about life, also about the afterlife. God so loved us, His children, that He made us for Himself eternally and proved that by His death and resurrection. Planting that seed-truth in the mind promis-es growth of hope with the passage of time on earth until death knocks at the door. When death knocks, grand ex-citement describes the believer's outlook.

The manager of a senior citizens home tells me dying for the Christian is entirely different than for the unbeliever. "As clear as night and day," he says. There are excep-tions, no doubt, due to medication or strange things that happen to the mind or one's conditioning. But the spir-itual law of hope is indeed law.

To encourage and grow in hope, one need only read from the hope literature of our time. Two examples:

Todd Burpo with Lynn Vincent. *Heaven Is for Real: A Little Boy's Astounding Story of His Trip to Heaven and Back.* Nashville: Thomas Nelson, 2010. That little fellow saw things in heaven he could not possibly have heard at his young age.

N. T. Wright. *Surprised by Hope: Rethinking Heaven, the Resurrection, and the Mission of the Church.* New York: HarperOne, 2008. One of the most inspiring and informed books I have read.

Interestingly, as we grow in hope and knowledge of heaven, life here on earth takes on more and more of the abundant life Jesus came to bring us. Jesus' word for *life* in the Gospel of John is always *zoe*, a rich term signaling fulfillment and abundance.

**Rekindled? Yes!**

\*\*\*              \*\*\*              \*\*\*

## WEEK'S SUMMARY POINT OF HOPE AND HEALING

**The word *Savior* means Healer; the term *salvation* means healing.**

# WEEK 3

# REKINDLED:

# THE HEALING POWER OF HUMOR

A joyful heart is good medicine,
but a crushed spirit dries up the bones.

—Proverbs 17:22 (ESV)

# Day 1

# HUMOR'S SOURCE

*Rx info-med*

Joy is the origin of the Christian's spirit of humor. "In the world you have tribulation," Jesus said with characteristic candor, "but be of good cheer, I have overcome the world" (John 16:33 RSV). The psalmist talks of God's anointing "with the oil of gladness" (45:7; cf. Heb. 1:9).

In joy lies strength: "The joy of the Lord is your strength" (Neh. 8:10b). Psalm 16:11 tells us that in God's presence "there is fullness of joy" and "pleasures for evermore."

Agnes Sanford discovered the relationship between joy and prayer in connection with the healing of her baby. Ill six weeks, the little one did not mend despite Mrs. Sanford's earnest intercessions. Then a young pastor came to pray. She thought his intercessions would do no good, but he insisted. When he talked to God, holding the baby in his arms, his eyes lighted up with sheer delight and Agnes believed. Joy, heaven's touch, unleashes the power of God. The baby fell asleep and awakened healed.

Reflecting on her earlier prayers, Agnes Sanford observed that she had allowed fear and desperation to grip her heart. These negatives had blocked her pleas.

I have friends who seem to say that cheer and humor grace life at every turn in life. Herein lies a basic principle of fulfilled living. With an enlightened spirit we pray over crucial issues to find faith's pathway to satisfying resolutions. God's gift of joy, from which laughter springs, oils the hinges to open doors freely into new light to see answers rich with possibilities.

When the flag waves over Buckingham Palace, the London home of Elizabeth II, the Queen is in residence. When the flag of joy waves in gentle breezes over His child, we know the Holy Spirit is in residence. Then laughter spills over the cup of joy and tumbles like a waterfall, signaling powerful therapy working against the threat of burnout.

### Rekindled? Yes!

# Day 2
## LAUGHTER IS THERAPY

### Rx info-med

Laughter is medicine. Norman Cousins famously discovered this truth for himself. Home from a working trip to Russia, he ended up in the hospital exhausted and very ill with a collagen disease. Little nodules formed under his skin. Some authorities gave Cousins only one in 500 chances (what the research indicated) to heal.

Fortunately, the physician, Dr. Hitzig, worked with Mr. Cousins, the two tailoring a therapy program. Cousins moved out of the hospital for privacy and put into gear the full exercise of affirmative emotions to enhance body chemistry. In addition to upbeat thinking and massive doses of vitamin C, laughter played a big role in recovery. Not that laughing proved easy: "Nothing is less funny than being flat on your back, with all the bones in your spine and joints hurting."

He met the pain challenge by systematically induced laughter, beginning with Allen Funt's *Candid Camera* films, then Marx Brothers' flicks:

> It worked. I made the joyous discovery that ten minutes of genuine belly laughter had an anesthetic effect and would give me at least two hours of pain-free sleep.… When the pain-killing effect of the laughter wore off, we would switch on the motion-picture projector again, and, not infrequently, it would lead to another pain-free sleep interval.

Sometimes the nurse read from humor books such as E. G. and Katherine White's *Subtreasury of American Humor* and Max Eastman's *The Enjoyment of Laughter.*

Did laughing really change his body chemistry? Did this extraordinary treatment actually help him get well? Norman Cousins answers:

> [W]e took sedimentation rate readings just before as well as several hours after the laughter episodes. Each time, there was a drop of at least five points. The drop by itself was not substantial, but it held and was cumulative.

Cousins' final conclusion? "I was greatly elated by the discovery that there is a physiologic basis for the ancient theory that laughter is good medicine."

The whole story eager readers will find in the fascinating book by Norman Cousins, *Anatomy of an Illness.* There he gives the full range of rich details connected with his successful therapy. Laughter played its role, effecting genuine cure.

By the same token, laughter plays its part not only in the cure of burnout but also in its prevention.

***Rekindled? Yes!***

# Day 3

## THE RELAXATION RESPONSE

### *Rx info-med*

The surrendered person lives at liberty to take life in stride and laugh at oneself.

My late friend Dr. James Moss, Professor of Orthodontics and head of his department at the University of London's College of Dentistry, packed an immense amount of work into his life. Past President of the National Society of Orthodontists, later president of the European division of a world orthodontics association, he traveled the globe presiding at meetings and sharing knowledge from his own surgical and research experiences.

Often people asked, "James, how do you do it all?" His reply came as easily as his work: "I just do it. I don't take myself seriously. People wear masks. They try to be perfect; they work so hard to get to the top. I don't care whether I get to the top." There we have his secret: "I don't care whether I get to the top." He said, "I'm just myself."

He is. Everybody feels comfortable around him. He wastes no energy hiding behind a self-protective and successful persona. Thus liberated, he serves with abandon not only as a dental surgeon and professor but also as father, husband, elder of his church, as well as lay preacher.

How do we stop taking ourselves with undue seriousness? How do we rid ourselves of the I've-got-to-make-it-to-the-top-rung-of-the-ladder posture that contributes to burnout?

The cartoonists help us laugh at ourselves, taking away the onus of awful *mustness.* Bill Watterson, famous for his humorous Calvin and Hobbes funny paper series (named after theologian John Calvin and philosopher Thomas Hobbes), knows how to unmask us. Pogo and Peanuts also did a good job at freeing us from ourselves. Today Pickles and Garfield help us in their own subtle ways. So do humorists such as P. G. Wodehouse. Perhaps one reason Wodehouse lived so long relates to his relaxed state of mind, creating his pompous figures at which we laugh with liberated delight. The London *Times* hailed Wodehouse a comic genius, calling him a master of farce. He died at ninety-three on Valentine's Day, 1975.

A good laugh may clear away early burnout feelings as morning sun burns off the soupy fog that engulfs us on our way to work.

Martin L. Gross, past editor of *Book Digest*, asked Erma Bombeck, "What does humor do for a person?" Aunt Erma's reply comes across as near classic:

> It does everything. It could save your life. It really could, particularly when you're faced with a situation that you think you just cannot handle. We've had that in our marriage situa-

tions. "Oh … we're never going to survive this." And then the humor comes back and says, "Hey, we're going to be OK" (Gross 28-29).

Yes, ok! Almost by magic.

### *Rekindled? Yes!*

# Day 4
## THE BEST WAY TO BE SERIOUS

*Rx info-med*

"The best way to get serious," observes an insightful man, "is to get humorous." He illustrates his point in the context of public speech.

"If you want an audience to take your message to heart, get them first to laugh." Laughter has a way of getting messages, sometimes very difficult messages, under our skin.

Laughter does more. It serves as a remarkably effective instrument for achieving dead serious goals. Humor puts people at ease in an atmosphere that gives birth to easy comprehension. Laughter triggers the flow of creative juices and puts the pieces of a puzzle together.

Without mirth, driving seriousness becomes malignant. A wise elder missionary statesman said to a fledgling missionary, "If you want to live awhile out here in Africa, learn to see the funny side of life." *Reader's Digest* had a point when it billed laughter as the "best medicine."

I asked a university president the secret of his longevity (he presided over three great institutions through several decades). "Humor," came his one-word reply. Humor enabled him to carry burdens lightly.

The comedic allows us to live with the contradictions of life. The person who must always act rationally kills creative possibilities with intensity. The over-intense embarrass themselves by their own contradictory behavior. People laugh at their frightening seriousness, but the too sober cannot laugh at themselves. To smile at one's inconsistency reveals the deepest consistency.

Humor allows us to live comfortably with ourselves, a significant clue to avoiding burnout. Perfectionism is the worst kind of seriousness, the poisoning that brings death to venturing out into creativity and innovation. *Rigor mortis* means demise of the spirit. Mirth is the antibiotic that heals the terribly rigid, thus releasing the inner person, restoring perspective, and turning on creativity with its accompanying productivity.

Sir James Barrie, in *Peter Pan*, Act I, tells us the origin of fairies: "When the first baby laughed for the first time, the laugh broke into a thousand pieces and they all went skipping about, and that was the beginning of fairies." In the same Act, Sir James comments, "Every time a child says, 'I don't believe in fairies' there is a little fairy somewhere that falls down dead." Glee gives rebirth to the fairy child in us all.

Psychologists remind us of the importance of keeping the child alive in us, for where else does freshness, wonder, excitement, the faith that accomplishes the impossible come from? An over-focused stance robs us of that inner child. "Do you believe in fairies?" asks Sir James Barrie in Act IV: "If you believe, clap your hands!"

How can serious adults facing the threat of burnout believe once more? Listen to Jesus about becoming a little child to enter the Kingdom of wholeness. See Him throw off the weight of Pharasaic criticism by the figure of speech "you are white-washed walls." Surely the common people broke up in sidesplitting laughter and heard Him gladly. Hear him talk about "the beam in the eye" as he uncovers the gross imperfections of people posing as perfect. Elton Trueblood found so much humor in our Lord that he wrote a whole book about it, *The Humor of Christ*. There was never a more wholesomely serious person than Jesus, who achieved goals, great and eternal goals, but without the overintensity that spells burnout.

### *Rekindled? Yes!*

# Day 5

# HUMOR GREASES THE WHEELS

### *Rx info-med*

"Not many humor books here, I'm afraid," lamented the librarian. She disappeared, returning in a few minutes with four or five books. She saw me forty minutes later visibly tickled as I read Morley and Leacock.

"Looks like you found something funny," she volunteered.

"Yes, and I'm trying to figure out how I can check out these books. I don't have my Library Card with me." Patiently she explained I would have to have the check-out card. I smiled knowingly and went on reading.

"Of course," she added as an afterthought, "if you're desperate I can give you a spring Bank Holiday emergency card."

"That would be nice," I replied to the gracious English lady, thinking, *humor's atmosphere persuades as little else can.*

The amusing Robert Morley offers his rich *Book of Worries*, an alphabetical listing of things that make us fret: age, baldness, blood pressure, cholesterol, clothes, dozens more. Any of Morley's farcically funny short pieces loosen tensions and release us in torrents of laughter—guaranteed!

The Stephen Leacock piece, "My Financial Career," I had not seen since youth when I read it in *Reader's Digest.* Now I laughed harder, the years interpreting the story's subtle nuances. I read it at home to Kathleen, and we both laughed till we cried. This little gem of an essay takes less than ten minutes to read but furnishes a day's therapy.

Work comes easier after sidesplitting humor. The machinery of the brain moves more smoothly. Hope makes its reentry quickly, quietly, almost unawares. Possibilities grow luminous. Artifice and, therefore, stress disappear.

When wheels squeak, apply the grease of humor.

**Rekindled? Yes!**

# Day 6
# A WAY OF SEEING

***Rx info-med***

Humorists win. They win because they see with laughter-corrected vision.

A novelist probably determined the success of his career because he used his good sense of humor as an agent for keeping his sight at 20/20. As a beginner reporter he got a letter from his father who wrote that his son would never amount to a hill of beans. Annoyed at his dad, he wrote that

> at 21 he did indeed seem incapable, but he had in fact thought out his life goal. His plan for achievement? At 30 he intended to be a great newspaper reporter; at 40 a great editor; at 50 a great story writer; at 60 a great fiction writer; at 70 a great grandfather; at 80 a great admirer of beautiful women; at 90 a great loss to the community.

His father had a good laugh. Significantly the years saw the son's career proceed along the very lines he predicted in that delightful letter.

I have a friend who refuses to worry. He knows worry fogs his lenses and confuses focus. My friend fought big problems for forty years but insisted on dissipating his anxiety potential in humor. Riotously funny, he reduces problems to a size easily manageable. He never allows them to tower over him to look down from some vague and apprehensive height. Humor becomes the spectacles through which he sees life. This way of seeing held him to faith and kept him collected through his long illness, then his wife's surgery. She now enjoys full health and together they relish retirement in Christian service overseas and at home.

The medical community knows that positive, beautiful thoughts create hormonal output in our bodies to help maintain good health, even to heal us. We know, too, that negative thinking and the belief that the world is basically bad, creates the opposite and issues in wear and tear on us, body, mind, and spirit.

Establish in your thinking the role of positive faith in generating light and life and promoting healthy hormonal flow.

And what generates this positive faith? Prayer, affirmative thinking, positive achievement, and, of course, humor. How do you look at your world? If through hostile, paranoid eyes, you can change your lenses, God being your ophthalmologist.

***Rekindled? Yes!***

# Day 7
## A WEAPON

*Rx info-med*

The Bible says, "Anxiety in a man's heart weighs him down" (Prov. 12:25). Scripture also observes that the things we fear come upon us (Job 3:25). When anxiety and fear bend the knee to laughter, delicious victory is very often our priceless possession.

Humor is God's weapon against fear and anxiety with their potential eventualities. A hijacker with a gun commanded passengers not to move. He entered the cockpit. While he was there, a professional comedian got everyone in the back laughing. When the hijacker returned to the cabin and saw all the people laughing, he concluded they did not take him seriously, lost his nerve, and gave up!

Hermon Jose, a TV comedian of a past generation and from Lisbon, Portugal, had great fun making light of political leaders. He aimed only at those who see the funny side of life. "Reagan tells jokes. Brezhnev does not. I leave the communists alone because they have no sense of humor." Jose knows that if people laugh they will survive and go on to victories. Those who cannot laugh have already mapped out their doom.

A doctor said of a friend, "He will never have a break-down because he has a hair-trigger laugh." Likewise, an insightful leader said of a colleague going through the stress of adjusting to retirement, "He laughs easily so I know he will come through this period of his life O.K." Humor opens the windows of our minds on reality and that sense of reality is mental health, wholeness.

One of the most interesting experiments in laughter re-search relates to alcoholism. The South African Brain Research Institute uses laughing gas, oxygen, and nitrous oxide. They note the reversal of both physical and psy-chological withdrawal symptoms accompanied by a shortening of detoxification periods in 700 subjects who received the treatment. The success rate is so high that some with expertise in the field of rehabilitation believe the treatment will become standard. (See South African Brain Research Institute—substance abuse and Nitrous Oxide. Web site.)

Another piece of good news: current research tells us body chemistry alters with laughter. Use it as a weapon against burnout.

**_Rekindled? Yes!_**

\*\*\*                  \*\*\*                      \*\*\*

## WEEK'S SUMMARY POINT OF
## HOPE AND HEALING

**Laughter does surgery on negative thoughts and ushers in joy and peace.**

# WEEK 4:

# REKINDLED: GENUINE SPIRITUALITY

Christ is the indispensable core of effective personal adjustment.

—Lawrence J. Crabb, Jr.
"Moving the Couch into the Church"
(*Christianity Today*, 22 Sept. 1978)

[God's] image is in us, however deeply buried
under the debris of our living,
and heaven is never beyond the reach of our fingers.

—Thomas Aquinas, *My Way of Life:
The Summa Simplified for Everyone*
by Walter Farrell and Martin J. Healy

# Day 1

# THE THERAPEUTIC POWER OF

# MORAL DECISIVENESS

## *Rx info-med*

A chief cause of burnout is inner conflict initiated and generated by indecisiveness. Indecisiveness may come to the surface when teased out by lifestyle challenges. For example, the Christian who thought he had his Judeo-Christian morality decided, learns of a church couple living together unmarried. They attend services now and then, do a bit of work for the church, even give money.

Or there's the committed Christian couple who leave their spouses and remarry. *Eros* has usurped *agape*; stimulus/response (often glandular) has usurped sacrificial love.

*They are such good people. Does God smile at them? Can one entertain a double standard?* All at once, one feels confused. Inner turmoil may result, even letting down one's personal behavioral convictions, only to find sooner or later emotional and spiritual pain. Turmoil and mental paralysis can result (see Rivadeneira 69).

Stability arises from secure footing. How do we come to grips with the threat of moral uncertainty? How do we keep the channels between us and God open to truth rather than waffling in the presence of so much moral grayness?

**Shake loose from the instabilities of the 60s.** The sexual revolution of the sixties and early seventies left its mark on North American society. The *Playboy* magazine arrived in 1953 with Marilyn Monroe as its first cover girl/centerfold. How easily we make excuses and find arguments in the culture, even in academic journals, to justify a *new morality*! Such questioning calls for taking fresh hold on the biblical standard. Study in depth specific scriptural passages (e.g., the Sermon on the Mount, Matthew 5-7, or Psalm 51 on David's confession after committing adultery with Bathsheba). Enrich and refine your Bible knowledge. Decide to make God's Word your foundation and reap the rich reward of security replete with freedom, joy, and health.

**Stay close to the Christ of the Gospels.** We have four Gospel accounts that tell us about Jesus of Nazareth. Modern scholarship shares a growing respect for these documents (e.g., Badham, also Bruce). The Christ of these dependable documents is our source of personal certainty.

**Remind yourself of the validation of Gospel truth— the resurrection of our Lord.** The resurrection of Jesus is God's way of saying, "What you see in Jesus is really true. This is My method of documentation." Doubting Thomas finally got that message as did the early Church. The resurrection fact establishes the certainty of Gospel doctrine and Kingdom ethics.

*Rekindled? Yes!*

# Day 2

## KEEP ON KEEPING ON

*Rx info-med*

Vigorous enthusiasm to keep on growing is a sound deterrent to burnout. Enlargement of spiritual knowledge and the increase of theological understanding do much to anchor us at deeper and deeper levels. What resources may we bank to help us?

**Silence.** God speaks in the quiet times—the middle of the night, early morning, over a sandwich at lunch, any time at all that the golden opportunity of solitude opens the door of mind and heart. Often God speaks not in the trumpet blast, nor even in the thunder of a great sermon, but in a still small voice.

Our listening skills continue to develop throughout life. Encourage those skills forward in discerning God's voice. Watch yourself grow in hearing capacity.

**The practice of Christian devotion.** Take a small section of Scripture, over against a big one, and ask questions: Do I understand this passage? Can I put it into practice? If I have put it into practice, can I do it better?

Follow the same deliberate pattern in reading the devotional classics—St. Francis, Thomas à Kempis, Brother Lawrence. Richard Foster's books, especially his anthologies of the Christian classics, provide best guidance in devotional reading (e.g., Foster and Smith). Foster's *Sanctuary of the Soul: Journey into Meditative Prayer* provides a wealth of guidance.

Thomas Oden's classic three-volume theology, now available in simplified form (one volume), will enlarge one's spiritual understanding to great profit.

**Association with growing Christians.** As you wrestle with the suffering going on inside you, find a sympathetic listening ear, especially someone mature in the faith. Dialog in all sincerity and find yourself moving up the ladder of spiritual experience and, therefore, comprehension, even healing.

Get into a small group of trusting disciples. Study, pray, share. Not only does fresh insight come in the group, but we also correct our misapprehensions when we listen to others. (See Billings, p.28, the graphic with these words from the article, "We should avoid interpreting the Bible alone. While sometimes the slogan '*sola scriptura*' is used to justify doing so, it is a serious distortion of that Protestant principle.")

**Say a resounding YES to the Spirit's call.** Dag Hammarskjold's classic response bears reading over and over again, always to our benefit:

> I don't know Who—or what—put the question, I don't know when it was put. I don't even remember answering. But at some moment I did answer Yes to Someone—or Something—and from that hour my life, in self-surrender, had a goal.

This surrender to God's call explains an Albert Schweitzer, a Raphael, or a Richard Baxter. In medical missions, painting, and preaching, these stalwarts got to the center of things. This arrival on center comes with no easy believism, but flowers as the result of honest and often prolonged grappling. The sense of wholeness that comes with giving oneself to the adventure God designs for us brings peace and joy unspeakable, what the Hebrews call *shalom.*

Amy Carmichael never stopped growing, never turned a deaf ear to the call to adventure. She rose to the challenge of mission in India where God assigned her work with young girls caught in the clutches of prostitution. During the last twenty years of her ministry, though invalided, she ran her girls' home from a bed! She realized that Life with a capital L results in saying yes to God's beckoning, whatever the cost. No wonder Billy Graham, upon visiting her Dohnavur home for girls, had to find a hiding place in the garden where he could weep privately. (Frank Houghton did a biography of Amy Carmichael. See Bibliography.)

*Rekindled? Yes!*

# Day 3
# WHO IS SPIRITUAL?

### *Rx info-med*

True spirituality is health, the ultimate answer to burnout. What makes a spiritual person?

**Love as lifestyle.** Novelist Fyodor Dostoyevsky, in *The Brothers Karamazov,* speaks through a character this way:

> At some ideas you stand perplexed, especially at the sight of men's sin, uncertain whether to combat it by force or by humble love. Always decide, 'I will combat it by humble love.' If you make up your mind about that once and for all, you can conquer the whole world. Loving humbly is a terrible force: it is the strongest of all things and there is nothing like it.

The word *love* appears something like half a hundred times in First John, the epistle that tells us that love of God and people is the test of spirituality. Jesus cried out against the eye-for-an-eye way of life and told His followers to relate to persons in the spirit of *agape* love which expresses consideration selflessly and sacrificially.

Write it down: Love is the first mark of the truly spiritual person.

**Progress.** St. Paul tells Timothy that Christians head for "righteousness, godliness, faith, love, steadfastness, gentleness" (1 Tim. 6:11). Jesus says His true disciples don't look back (Luke 9:62; Heb. 6:4). Intentional Christians endure to the end (Matt. 24:12-13; I Tim. 6:12–contrast v. 9). They also run to win the prize (1 Cor. 9:24-27). Christians go places and do things in service for Christ and His children. Spiritual persons do not live aimlessly but dream of grand Kingdom goals.

**Freedom, joy, and authority come from submission.** The one yielded to God is the spiritual person. The unsurrendered may become the burned-out person without authority over self or ability to relate confidently to others. Open and humble submission to the Almighty matures one into self-hood, and with it comes His peace, security, and freedom.

Only God can remake us. To try to create a new self ends only in frustration. Submit to God who will provide personal liberty, initiative, and creative insight to relate fully to Him, others, and oneself. In that confident relating lies true spirituality and fulfillment.

*Rekindled? Yes!*

# Day 4

# THREE FLAGS

*Rx info-med*

F. W. Faber, spiritual giant of the past, raised warning flags for the individual earnest about the spiritual life: prayer, suffering, and action. Look at these three through the lens of your own life and time.

*Prayer* gets at the heart of our religious life. Sigmund Freud believed religion was escapist and, therefore, ultimately invalid. Many, taking their clue from Freud, believe prayer an escape from reality. Let's face it: Some do indeed use supplication as a device for avoiding the challenges of life. But avoidance praying can make one sick because the pray-er uses intercession as a substitute for embracing reality, a cover for hiding the truth. Artifice never leads to authentic praying. All escapist thinking sends us the very conflict that creates burnout.

While Carl Jung said much religion shows signs of sickness, he came to believe faith a significant factor in health and healing. Sincere, believing praise, intercession, and petition help to prevent and contribute toward healing burnout.

*Suffering* presents its own challenges. Carl Jung, in the 1930s, observed that "about a third of my cases are suffering from no clinically definable neurosis, but from the senselessness and emptiness of their lives. It seems to me that this can well be described as the general neurosis of our time." That statement strikes us as astonishingly current and relates aptly to many a burned-out soul.

The real threat of suffering relates to our fear of its potential—dropping us into the abyss of uselessness. But by God's help we will not fall, only rise to daily challenges as stepping-stones to meaningful work and living. Suffering is the soil in which seeds of fulfillment sprout, develop, and flower.

Eager readers will find one of the best sources for documenting this grand truth in Lettie B. Cowman's *Streams in the Desert.* She put that book together while her husband suffered through four years of painful cardiac issues that eventually took his life. He had helped establish the Oriental Missionary Society's church in both Japan and Korea. Overwhelmed with suffering, he seemed stranded, helpless in following the Lord's call.

Today that mission organization, now known as One Mission Society, covers much of the globe with thousands of churches. And for further documentation that Romans 8:28 proves true, note that *Streams in the Desert* continues to circulate nonstop through many printings and over a vast territory. Few devotional books can match it for readership.

The flag called suffering must not become a stumbling block, but a door to healing and wholeness.

*Action* looks so terribly good in an action-oriented socie-ty, yet here we must wave the caution flag in full view. When flashy and forward, doing reflects what Shake-speare called "much ado about nothing"; more, it can be-come mere ego-tripping. (A medical student told me one of her professors warned against over-treating.) Let mo-tivation find its roots in the Word and works of God, and the resulting action will take on divine meaning. Postur-ing lacks full-orbed purpose; helping a fellow human be-ing takes on the fullest kind of meaning. The Bible story reveals God Himself in action, and His actions in Christ give us the clue to the kind of helping action born in heaven.

The subconscious mind detects artificiality but also au-thenticity. The one sets up conflict and, therefore, the road to burnout; the other constructs the road to servant-hood, which creates in one's very soul the peace that passes all understanding as well as deep satisfaction.

IN SUMMARY, three flags—prayer, suffering, and ac-tion—represent both threat and opportunity. Take oppor-tunity, with its manifold possibilities, and walk the road to wholeness.

**Rekindle? Yes!**

# Day 5

## PRAYER'S IMPERATIVE

### *Rx info-med*

God is for the desperate, said a man who understands how the Gospel works. The Almighty cannot answer requests that say, "I think I can handle this myself," or "If I find resolution to my problem, I can explain it on natural grounds." A good deal of what we discover about the secrets of intercession and petition comes out of genuine crises such as burnout.

To admit a crisis and to face our helplessness opens the door to His grace and moderates that inner conflict that leads to burnout.

Part of the answer to mounting frustration, then, lies in complete dependence. Sincere obedience to His will brings surrender, which sees prayers answered in divine timing. Genuine asking brings genuine answering.

Facing crises in solid dependence has a way of demanding something specific from us. Jesus asked persons in need, "What do you want me to do for you?" "Lord, we want our eyes opened." Particularized asking brings particularized answering.

Children figured significantly in Jesus' ministry because they ask in pristine sincerity. Who can say no to childlike faith? Jesus sees God as a father responding to us with good gifts, not stones for bread or serpents for fish (Matt. 7:9-10). The Father/child relationship says God is Creator and Sustainer. He has at His disposal all I need. He's ready to give when I'm ready to ask.

The hang-up relates to our conditioning that renders us incapable of thinking like little children. The saints declare in absolutely clear terms, "Of course you cannot make yourself a child, nor 'have' faith." That very admission is God's first grip on the knob of your heart's door. He walks through the door into our hearts with gift after gift.

And if the fog of burnout and confusion seems to lock the door? The Psalmist evidently wrestled and struggled because in desperation he cries, "Answer me when I pray…." God does answer him, for the writer of Psalm 4 says triumphantly, "When I was in trouble you helped me" (v. 1 TEV).

The secret? Dependence despite desperation.

***Rekindled? Yes!***

# Day 6
## GOD'S TIME

### *Rx info-med*

One of the causes of suffering and breakdown relates to forcing oneself to live patiently with a problem. There's a better way than self-compulsion.

I once heard a bishop say he prayed nine years for the solution to a crucial concern. From the glow on his face and the tone in his voice as he preached, every listener knew that his long course in the school of prayer brought its reward.

How should we view the long wait?

**Note the frequency of the word *wait* in Scripture.** Over and over again the Psalms tell us to wait (e.g., 25:5; 31:4; 130:5-6). As we wait for the Lord He sustains us, and in His own time answers our heart cries.

The clear Bible teaching? God answers in His *kairos* time (i. e., just the right time). Jesus the Messiah appeared on earth after centuries of waiting—in the fulfillment of time God sent Jesus. Just so God answers our prayers in His hour, His time. That basic knowledge brings the hope called anticipation.

**See the plight as our advantage.** When we do not get quick answers, when answers seem forever coming, we feel helpless, stranded. But God, even when we cannot sense it, has special concern for the helpless. To learn to live at God's pace takes time.

The god who helps those who help themselves actually proves helpless. Pagan do-it-yourself religion results in disappointment. Yet this very attitude sometimes lives in the guise of Christian faith and spirituality. Other times it crops up as unabashed humanism, even in the Christian church.

True, we are incarnational Christians, God and humans working together. Classical theology teaches that God Himself takes the initiative, planting within us capacities for doing. Yes, we must cooperate (God made us with free will), but the gifts required to accomplish good things start and continue with Him. This explains why so often people who look incapable become astonishingly capable. D. L. Moody used atrocious English, but no one can rob him of his place in the history of effective public preaching.

So does God take His time equipping us? Do we need to wait for that maturation process to come to the proper point in time? Waiting has a way of forming a larger picture in our minds and hearts.

**Waiting does something else—it helps us live with realistic perspective.** A long wait puts us in touch with bedrock fact. Compelled to analyze, examine, figure, wrestle and wonder, we sift through possibilities, eliminate misconceptions, and little by little come to grips with a picture that is good, true, and beautiful.

Singles must think twice before marrying; how many stories of tragedy could have come to happy fruition! Young believers need to evaluate their calling and giftedness. It is not a good thing to jump into an ill-fitting job. Older folks do well to evaluate their circle of friends. A good church brings untold blessings—it can lead to quality friends.

**We thank God His plan will succeed**. Deeply spiritual people testify to the role of praise in patient suffering. And often waiting is a suffering business. Gratitude has releasing power, a fact revealed in Scripture and increasingly confirmed by modern brain research. Positive thoughts trigger chemical output, which factors into changing a person's outlook. With new insight all kinds of possibilities and creative options offer themselves for the cure of burnout.

*Rekindled? Yes!*

# Day 7
# REALIZING DREAMS

*Rx info-med*

Frustrated dreams cause burnout. Fulfilled dreams bring grand relief. God favors good visions.

We do well to remind ourselves that God Himself puts great pictures into our minds. He works through sanctified motivations to let us know when we veer from His best plan. Let His noble goals develop in your thinking.

As you allow God's dream to imprint itself on your brain, you will, with His direction, fill in the blanks. But first comes the outline, the broad strokes of the painting. Then details take their proper form.

For example, suppose you sense an urge to pursue a graduate degree for personal growth and the improvement of your professional skills. Look first at where to study, what specific discipline to capture your attention, and with whom to research. Exploration guided by earnest prayer will show you the way.

Allow yourself to see God's biggest, grandest picture for you. Big dreams draw the best out of us. The more demanding the vision the more it will ask of you, and the more it asks, the more productive the achievement. And the more demanding the personal investment, the more satisfying the result.

Pray for grace to liberate yourself from comfortable ruts. In youth, great dreams do not seem so formidable as in later years when the wear and tear of life threatens to knock the cutting edges off aspiring designs. Even when you have the job and the house for which you planned and longed for so long, you now need new expectations, for without a vision you perish (Prov. 29:18). An exciting image of future service will create the makings of high adventure, and in that very risk lies powerful therapeutic resources.

Pray for grace to sustain enthusiasm to see your vision come to its most complete and beautiful flowering. Brace yourself with the whole armor of God for coping with challenges that attack your plan, for no worthy dream goes uncontested. In the energy of the Divine, receive your new goal, then watch God bring your dreams to fruition.

***Rekindled? Yes!***

＊＊＊        ＊＊＊                    ＊＊＊

## WEEK'S SUMMARY POINT OF
## HOPE AND HEALING

**God motivates and refreshes sincere, persistent, spiritually-oriented believers.**

# WEEK 5

# REKINDLED: STRESS AND DISTRESS

[M]ost of our tensions and frustrations stem from compulsive needs to act the role of someone we are not. Only he who knows himself can profit by the advice of Matthew Arnold: "Resolve to be thyself: and know that he who finds himself, loses his misery."

—Hans Selye, M.D.
*The Stress of Life*

Come to me, all who labor and are heavy laden,
and I will give you rest. Take my yoke upon you,
and learn from me; for I am gentle and lowly in heart,
and you will find rest for your souls.
For my yoke is easy, and my burden is light.

—Matt. 11:28-30, RSV

# Day 1
# DEFINING STRESS

*Rx info-med*

Hans Selye discovered and documented chemical-biologic involvement in stress, such as adrenal enlargement, increase of corticoids in the blood, and weight loss.

75

Stress, with its biological components, is normal, even needed to get a job done.

Our challenge does not relate so much to stress as to distress. The real provocation lies in discovering why certain activities frustrate us and how to use and win over them. Finding a workable answer to that crucial question makes living not only bearable but vibrant with productivity.

The fundamental clue lies in self-identity. Pretending you are something you are not raises the stress quotient. You can overtax yourself very quickly by pretending. Genuine closeness to God facilitates self-identity. The work of the Spirit relates to showing us our gifts and graces, where we fit, and also to adjusting and shaping us to fit where He sends us. Our Maker knows us—better than we know ourselves—and empowers us to be just ourselves.

We must cooperate with the Spirit in the work of identifying our gifts. Developing skills commensurate with personal talents may take awhile, and surely when we enter a new field of endeavor we find ourselves in the throes of freshly identifying ourselves. Our culture may lead us astray, for eagerness to succeed can take precedence over prayerful focus on our personal gifts. The flashy charismatic gifts can deceive, even warp us. Calm and collected people do not attempt to be something they are not.

Style itself factors into defining oneself. Some work with great speed; others achieve goals at a more deliberate pace. Many a gifted person labors quietly, unobtrusively;

others consult authorities and associates with a lot of verbal and bodily presence. Discover your own life and work style, cutting off unnecessary concomitants and adding other bits and pieces articulating with who you are. Once you find your own comfortable modicum of operation, tension tends to disappear.

Here, then, lies a law of de-stressing: We flourish when we sense work lies within the framework of our developing gifts, graces, talents, and style. When work, goals, and style mesh, fulfillment results.

### *Rekindled? Yes!*

# Day 2
# SELF-ACCEPTANCE

### *Rx info-med*

Self-identity comes with difficulty in our Wall Street culture. The world, saturated with advertisements both bold and subtle, calls us to change. Some changes benefit us while other modifications confuse us or prove impossible.

Researchers tell us that on any single day, dozens if not hundreds, even thousands, of advertising messages bombard us (an estimated range of 150 to 3,000). We hear urgent suggestions to dress a certain way, use a particular cosmetic to transform our appearance, or go to a hair stylist who will make us appealing. The subtle implication is that we are not all we could or should be. Dissatisfaction sets in, followed by an attempt to remake ourselves. With such an attempt we may enjoy a brief period of satisfaction, but soon we see ourselves in need of another redo.

Advertising philosophy builds on idealized and marketing assumptions. Flawless-skinned beauties adorn magazine covers; shiny automobiles appear in show windows; impeccably dressed men come onto our TV screens. American idealism does not fit the reality of hard-driving work days. We must learn to pierce perfectionistic conditioning to see ourselves as real people. Perfectionism, a disease the counselor often deals with, can produce distress and even burnout.

We must find what we can do well—not perfectly—and proceed to develop gifts to the full. Learn to live with yourself as you are and where you are, knowing that everyone is in process. Those who live comfortably with themselves know the secret of avoiding distress. In that living and working context, maturation takes place as naturally as blossoms precede tiny green fruit, which in turn becomes ripe-ready food for the dinner table.

Fruit blossoms initially look quite a bit alike, but in time the pear, peach, and cherry define themselves. God accepts your age and stage at this moment in time. Refuse the temptation to think that your past is worse or better than the present. Believe in your future; for with the Christian, hope flowers into beautiful skills with accompanying achievement.

### *Rekindled? Yes!*

# Day 3

# REDUCING STRESS BY

# MEDITATION AND RELAXATION

### *Rx info-med*

Consider three techniques, any one of which may well de-stress over-taxed people.

**Visualization.** Recall any joyous scene from your memory bank. I like water and can see in my mind's eye Lake Lucerne, Switzerland, near which our family vacationed years ago. The serenity of the lake's surface, the happy walking trails under spreading branches along the waterfront, the snow-covered mountains in the distance—such a picture brings a welcome peace all its own, making me feel happy and secure.

The Gospel pictures provide an ancient resource for visual meditation. Read the spiritual heroes of the faith—St. Francis, Augustine, Thomas à Kempis, et al, and notice the vast amount of pictorial material—the cross, empty tomb, the healing of the blind man Bartimaeus. If you choose the Resurrection of our Lord, see the stone rolling away, Jesus emerging, then standing in all His radiance in front of the empty tomb.

As you meditate, notice your problems fading and tension diminishing. Relaxation quickly sets in.

This visualization technique, employed by ancients and moderns, proves helpful to many contemporaries wrestling with the hassles of living. The secret lies in the quiet collection of your mind. The chosen vignette captures your imagination, brings peace, and transports you to another world.

**Step-by-step relaxation.** Sit in a straight chair, feet flat on the floor, arms dangling. Turn the radio or TV off, as well as the phone. Still your total person. Become perfectly quiet.

Now relax beginning at the top of your head, moving to your forehead, eyes, cheek bones, chin. Then see yourself relieve tension in shoulders, upper arms, elbows, lower arms, and hands. Move on to torso, midriff, upper and lower legs, then feet. In your mind, slowly let each part of your anatomy submit to perfect relaxation. Let muscle strands lengthen into inactivity. Having achieved slackening from head to toe, remain in perfect repose for several minutes.

Take advantage of this tranquility to invite the Spirit of Jesus freshly into your total being. Sense Him enter every fiber of your person. Stay quietly with Him, following the admonition of Psalm 46:10: "Be still and know that I am God."

This unhurried technique acts as a tranquilizer. It provides new mental agility for a day's work, a clear mind for decision making in the throes of grappling with a knotty problem, and preparation for a good night's sleep.

**Centering.** The Quakers talk about *centering down*, the process of clearing the mind of busyness to give heed to the Inner Voice. Worshiping with Friends in the old Quaker town of Saffron Walden, England, I discovered centering takes about twelve minutes in a group setting. After that quieting period, someone often shares a message from God.

Try centering in your prayer group. You may surprise yourself and your prayer partners with the messages that come in the grand context of serenity. And heaven's messages, with their inevitable fresh perspectives, go a long way toward de-stressing a person.

Do centering in your own private devotion. After ten minutes or so, you will begin to hear God speak. Remember that the quietness itself is God speaking, gracing you with the message, actually the reality, called *rest*.

Saintly people have used *centering prayer* for generations. An ancient prayer, "Lord Jesus, have mercy on me," repeated over and over, can serve to bring you into fresh and healthy focus. In such prayer the personality pulls together, collected, centered down, and integrated.

### *Rekindled? Yes!*

# Day 4
# MUSIC AND THE ARTS

### *Rx info-med*

The arts have a way of taking us beyond ourselves. The reason, of course, lies in imagination, what someone has called the sixth sense. The sensory part of us works to transport us into the world of story, beauty, deep feelings, "aha" moments of insight and vibrant life.

A stressed restaurateur in Greece told me, "After work I go home to listen to some classical music." A college professor of Greek and Latin observed that a concert can "rest you" after a hard day's work. A bookstore manager reads novels at night.

Art lovers find themselves absorbed in canvases by Monet, Rembrandt, and Constable—the museum becomes a restoration place, a kind of hospital to the stress-worn. Substance, color, shape, distance, and especially light become healing instruments.

Any of the arts have power to carry us away from ourselves and our hectic world, setting us down in an entirely new context. Painting, dance, and literature stimulate the imagination to saunter down memory lanes, creating enriched desire for invention, innovation, or exploration.

Pablo Casals, the famous cellist who also played piano, sat at the keyboard first thing each morning. He suffered from twisted arthritic hands, but once into Bach or Beethoven, his fingers loosened and stretched out into near normal. Music is therapy, and its power to transport our thoughts into a whole new world plays into that healing and release.

Now for a proviso. Noisy music like heavy metal can penetrate with its cacophonous sounds into the psyche, adding stress upon stress to usher in still more distress. Evaluate your ear, test yourself against discordant music, classical or rock, loud jazz forms or incessant drum beat. Lay alongside that evaluation other *noisy* expressions of art. The following funny story is a metaphor for testing what kinds of artistic expression distress you.

> Liz, a senior citizen, is on her first-ever visit to an art gallery. She sees a huge black canvas splattered with yellow paint blobs, and next to it a murky gray canvas streaked with purple paint drips.
>
> Puzzled, Liz approaches the artist and says, "Excuse me, sir. I don't understand your paintings."
>
> "I paint what I feel inside me," the artist replies.
>
> "Oh, I'm sorry," says Liz. "Have you ever tried Alka-Seltzer?"

We smile at that little bit of humor, but it suggests something about appraising art forms that help or hinder handling distress. Sometimes we need lighter fare like elevator music or a Thomas Kinkade painting.

Another part of the caution: Cognitive music (J. S. Bach, Haydn, Mozart) rests the spirit of some but disturbs others. In addition, depending on one's mood or mind-set, music requiring a high level of perception may fatigue rather than calm. Classical jazz has great diversionary powers, releasing one from the wear and tear of the day. But not always. The bottom line is, exercise freedom to choose the kind of music that fits at the moment. The same principle applies to reading—a hair-raiser of a detective novel may not work like the poetry of Wordsworth, Coleridge, or Angelou. Viewing a jarring social awareness play on PBS may not do the job like Tchaikovsky's Swan Lake ballet.

## *Rekindled? Yes!*

# Day 5

# THE BODY AND MIND NEED DIVERSIONS

### *Rx info-med*

My friend Joe did not like what the doctor told him. His wife had contracted a rare disease that would rob her of body movement and lucidity. The physician prognosticated correctly. Joe put on his thinking cap, figuring out a way to take care of his lifelong companion while at the same time caring for himself. Wisely, he hired a student one day a week to stay with his wife so he could play at his favorite sport, golf. His day out in the fresh air and on the greens with his cronies, proved a major factor in his own well-being, thus helping to sustain himself through the final days of her life.

A seminary president suffered high blood pressure. The doctor ordered him to visit nearby mountain streams periodically. Interestingly, when he went to the clinic after the fishing episodes, his blood pressure read normal.

Hans Selye, the famous Canadian cardiologist and stress researcher, rode a bicycle. He de-stressed by vigorous outdoor exercise and kept himself physically fit. I personally find daily swimming a refreshing escape from the tensions of life. The pool enhances my appetite, results in deepened sleep, clears the brain, and keeps the cardiovascular system intact.

Including regular exercise into your schedule will contribute to keeping mind, body, and emotions in working order.

Andrea Wulf, in her book *Founding Gardeners: The Revolutionary Generation, Nature, and the Shaping of the American Nation*, reveals what came to me as a big surprise. George Washington, Thomas Jefferson, John Adams and others of our founding fathers eased their anxieties by gardening. Agriculture played a large part in their lives. They loved the soil, read books on how to advance crop productivity, and wrote letters to each other about trees, garden design, acreage, and its cultivation. Washington, in the throes of preparing for the crucial battle of New York, cornered himself in privacy to write not so much about the upcoming skirmish as about his gardening and agricultural endeavors. In this way he calmed his mind in preparation for designing victory in the upcoming conflict (13-14).

And what about diversions such as board games? A busy doctor played checkers one evening a week with a clergy friend. A Harvard Biblical scholar wrote detective stories in between working with colleagues on a fresh translation of the New Testament.

"All work and no play makes Jack a dull boy." Also a very distressed boy. Conversely, diversionary play makes Jack a de-stressed boy.

### Rekindled? Yes!

# Day 6

## WORK GOD'S WAY

### *Rx info-med*

Mother Teresa counsels us to work without vanity and pride, for after all, we're engaged in *God's* Kingdom enterprise: "Put yourself completely under the influence of Jesus." In *A Gift from God,* she goes on to warn us that we quickly fall into the trap of working for the sake of work. But we work for God, for Christ, and that means we endeavor to labor in beautiful, fulfilling ways.

This temptation to work for the sake of working, with its sneaky infiltrating power and the promise of more money, can take us unwittingly away from the presence and power of God. Just there stress sets in. How do we implement Mother's Teresa's pattern of work?

**Stay close to the living Christ.** Find an isolated place— one person drives to the ocean and parks; another enters a cathedral; still another goes to a retreat center. I personally have a room in my home to which I go early each morning.

Once you have found your spot, silence your mind in the presence of Christ. Ask Him to saturate every centimeter of your being.

**Know that Christ lives and breathes in you.** Frank C. Laubach shared in the little book, *Letters by a Modern*

*Mystic,* how this awareness became reality for him. He told of the stress he experienced working with half a million hostile Moros in the Philippines. Laubach, in the Spirit's takeover, turned the frustration that could easily have become burnout into an astonishing and victorious missionary enterprise.

Laubach's great victory came when he visualized Christ talking through his lips, helping through his hands, walking with his legs, smiling with his face. He realized with the newness of a glorious early morning that Jesus actually made him a vehicle of His communication.

### *Rekindled? Yes!*

# Day 7

## GUILT-FREE ESCAPE

***Rx info-med***

A surprise letter came with these words:

> I will be working through my contractual year. I don't know
> what I'll do then. I am really tired of having nonstop respon-
> sibilities, so I am taking a leave of absence. I may go on full-
> time staff at the county social services. I have applied for a
> similar job in a nearby county too. I am looking forward to
> having a job I can go home from.

The frustrated man continues:

> The place where I work has been more than generous to me
> since my arrival. I heartily recommend this place to any one
> who is excited and fired up, ready to go to it. I just don't
> have it anymore. I would like to return to school but finances
> will not permit that.… I will appreciate your prayers as I
> seek God's will.

He complains about long working hours, adding, "I'm
ready for a leisurely soak in a tub of hot water. I think
every muscle is crying."

Clearly this man suffers distress, not mere stress. Credit
him for showing wisdom in seeking a way out of his misery. His intense concentration on professional goals over
a long period of time has resulted in a lopsided stress
quotient. He does not need someone to tell him to quit
complaining; he must get another job (sometimes good)
or, preferably, learn the art of diversification in order to

eliminate his stress now morphed into distress. How should he proceed?

**He must learn to hear his own cry.** The inner monitor tries to inform one of the need for relief. The letter writer did not hear because of the daily busyness that drowned out inner messages. His spouse may have tried to help him listen. Symptoms probably included a lack of interest in anything but work, blaming others for his mistakes, complaining about work load, lack of energy, and a sense of helplessness. This man, whether he continues in his first profession or changes to social services, will do well to learn how to listen to his basic needs.

**He would be smart to initiate a program of diversions: racquetball, Agatha Christie detective novels, hobbies, traveling, whatever.** He may need to experiment. If one activity does not get his mind off work, the diversion may become a new irritant, another emotional failure. A pastor suffering hypertension took up stamp collecting at the suggestion of his doctor. That was years ago and now, decades later and in retirement, he pastors a Presbyterian Church with delight and amazing health for his age.

**A trick one will want to remember: develop guilt-free escapes before symptoms appear.** Some walk a lot, like the tribal people of the South African veldt. They also talk with each other, while walking in pairs or small clusters, to the point of catharsis. While walking and talking, they enjoy the out-of-doors with its deep blue sky, its wild banana trees, and its rondovals.

Those of us living in urban settings need to build something of this relaxed lifestyle in our own cultural context and into our weekly, if not daily, round. In this way we will enjoy a healthy measure of relief from the pressures of life and work.

### *Rekindled? Yes!*

\*\*\*              \*\*\*              \*\*\*

## WEEK'S SUMMARY POINT OF
## HOPE AND HEALING

**Loving my neighbor as myself frees me to be myself.**

# WEEK 6

# REKINDLED: THE THERAPY OF CREATIVITY

> A man is never truly himself except
> when he is actively creating something.
>
> —Dorothy Sayers
> *A Matter of Eternity*

## Day 1

## CREATIVITY AS MEDICINE

*Rx info-med*

Norman Cousins, in *The Anatomy of an Illness*, painted pictures of two of his friends, Pablo Casals and Albert Schweitzer. Casals, almost ninety and bent with arthritis, took his medicine called "piano and cello." In the morning he played the piano, in the afternoon the cello. Cousins watched stiff fingers become agile and powerful. Casals' back straightened to more erect posture, his walk lost its shuffle. Ailments yielded to the body's cortisone and adrenaline. Blood pressure increased, bringing new vitality to mind and body.

Albert Schweitzer believed the sense of meaning he realized from his job as a missionary doctor, along with humor, played a significant role in keeping illness away. Disease found little hospitality in his body. Even after age ninety, Dr. Schweitzer did hospital rounds and involved himself in strenuous manual labor. He loved playing Bach on the piano at the end of a full day. After playing, Norman Cousins observed, the old gentleman had "no trace of a stoop. Music is his medicine."

Creativity and a deep sense of purpose go together. Clearly the one influences the other, but *how* still remains one of the great ongoing research challenges of our time. Why do we respond excitedly to stimuli? We know that vitality and chemistry relate. Scientists also know about the adrenal system, the pituitary gland, brain impulses, and the body's endocrine program. The accumulation of data grows.

At the experiential level, we know from observation that stimuli big enough to draw the best out of us bring a grand sense of fulfillment and often issue in results very helpful to the workplace, even to the wider community.

Creativity is medicine, medicine effective both to prevent burnout and to cure it.

### Rekindled? Yes!

# Day 2
## GETTING ORIGINAL

### *Rx info-med*

One of the delicious opportunities of life is to find innovative ways to do the job at hand.

C. S. Lewis tells us not to try to be original but to follow the truth as we see it with integrity and do the task assigned with conscientious care. Then a breakthrough happens—we end up being original! Not that we imitate someone else's creativity and pretend that it's ours, nor that we necessarily do the job after a prescribed formula. The clue is to labor in response to your individual impulses. Looking for originality, says Lewis, spoils it. Doing our best work, with no thought of *being ingenious* to get noticed, results in the uniqueness that mirrors the special person God made.

Imitation has its place, but only as a precursor to one's own creative output. I watched young painters in Rome, learning the principles of depiction by copying works of the masters. But principles and creativity are two quite different things. Yes, the one is essential to the other, yet when the laws of art find their expression in the nuances of one's own personality, fruit-bearing singularity springs to life.

Why do we know James Galway's sound almost instantly when we turn on the classical music station and hear a flute concerto played by him? He follows the rules—notes, rests, tone, breathing, etc. But he pours into his sound that distinctive component we know only as James Galway the original.

Mechanics do play a part, a kind of undergirding for artistic expression. My friend Virginia Brubaker, a professional pianist, began her studies very young. Her teacher corrected mistakes, made suggestions about volume and flow. The teacher did a good job instructing in the techniques of piano performance. Virginia appreciated this guidance, but while still a teenager, she determined to please her instructor by an impeccably perfect rendition of an assigned score. She worked assiduously, and come time for the display of her rehearsed composition, her piano coach listened with admiration, but with one caveat: "I would like to hear you play that number years later after you have suffered awhile."

Accepting oneself as an original at the hand of God and embracing the bottlenecks in the road to achievement bring creative productivity that will surprise you when it comes. And when it arrives, you will enjoy deep satisfaction and a measure of relief from burnout.

### *Rekindled? Yes!*

# Day 3

# THE DELIGHTS OF AFTERNOON TEA

## *Rx info-med*

Novelist Henry James gave us a near-proverb saying: "There is nothing quite so delightful as the custom of afternoon tea." Kathleen and I do afternoon tea and have done so for many years. Our stay in the United Kingdom fixed the four o'clock habit. And it is indeed delightful.

We often invite guests, who always come with joy to our little island of relaxed conversation accompanied by the tickling of the taste buds and the ticking of the grandfather clock in the corner. In this atmosphere of peace and joy, *of letting go*, the brain seems to originate not only the happiest of conversations but often quite remarkable comments, comments that provide unexpected information or bridges from one idea to another—even bits and pieces of knowledge put into fresh configurations of truth.

Little children show this same kind of sparkle. Their questions sometimes amuse us: "Daddy, who made God? Mommy, why does the water go down the bathtub drain one way and not the other?" Who would not like to be like a child and ask questions, questions that may materialize into an invention, a new way of doing chores, or an original program for executing homework? Or just an innocent way of seeing life?

I once asked a seasoned inventor what ideas commandeered his thinking at the moment. "Oh," he said, "a big percentage of invention is *thinking about what ought to be invented.* So I never tell anyone what I'm working on." Inventive minds ask questions few if any have thought of.

We need to make provision for thinking outside the box, whether at afternoon tea with stimulating friends, or in the shower, or while gardening. Actually, associating with children helps, for carefree thinking is contagious.

Sometimes brainstorming inspires creativity and innovation:

> What would happen if we moved the computers to the other end of the office?
>
> Do you suppose work efficiency would elevate if we played classical music rather than Rock over the intercom? (Actually, we have research on that question. Work does go better with classics and grades go up in school with kids who bathe their brains in Bach, Beethoven, and Brahms.)
>
> What would happen if we had a quiet half day a week, even away from the office, to cogitate about how to enhance our efficiency? (Some companies do that sort of rescheduling, resulting in remarkable efficiency and productivity.)

A college president told me that Lloyd contributed much to his administrative group sessions. I knew Lloyd well and viewed him, like most everyone did, as a fine intellect who asked questions, knotty questions, too, and sometimes questions no one else could think of. He irritated some, but not this college president who saw possibilities emerging from Lloyd's fearless interrogations.

Garden-fresh thoughts, coupled with the resultant sense of well-being, provide remarkable therapy and a wall protecting eager workers against burnout.

**Rekindled? Yes!**

# Day 4

# MEMORY, IMAGINATION,

# INTELLECT AND ACTION

### *Rx info-med*

These four gifts of the Creator are replete with possibilities. But possibilities can be both negative and positive, both debilitating and grand.

**Inviting Beautiful Memories.** Building a select memory bank is one of the invaluable opportunities of human beings as parents know. The family that travels together not only stays together (as families who sing and pray together) but also fills little memory banks with beautiful, meaningful, and informative pictures. In Europe castles and palaces, cathedrals and churches, rivers and lakes make their memorable and, therefore, imaginative impact. The intercultural experiences leave their mark, as do the historical spin-offs of international travel.

Family times at Thanksgiving and Christmas leave unforgettable impressions on us all, young and old. Laughter, storytelling, political talk, questions about food preparation, and gifts—they can only leave vivid pictures in the storehouse of the mind. And good pictures, provided they come packaged in happy, positive, and upbeat wrappings.

To the contrary, pornography, gossip, bitter wrangling—these things disease the memory. Many a person, with a background of poor conditioning, turns into a complainer, an habitually angry man, or a lust-warped woman.

**Watch Memory Turn into Imagination.** Make the memory bank rich in deposits, then watch it yield! Watch it morph into glad dreaming.

> That trip I took to Europe—I could study there.
>
> The magnificent Christmas concert I attended last year—what if I would go to the choral concert again this season?
>
> That English professor who encouraged me—what an adventure if I would do graduate studies in literature?

The dreams come! But if the memory bank is terribly soiled, the soul suffers haunting nightmares and prompts negative and questioning self-talk.

> That pornographic scene—dreaming of that kind of behavior translates into frightening imaginative canvases on the brain.
>
> That gossip lifestyle I grew up with—that could warp me interpersonally.
>
> Those complainers, sadly some of them Christians, could taint the wholesome influence I want to have.

Facing these potential downers, I firmly decide to entertain positive, not negative, dreams.

**Thinking Through My Dreams.** Processing our memories opens doors rich in possibilities.

> The Christmas choral concert would enrich my knowledge of sung music, bring joy to my spirit, and grace me with a delightful socializing opportunity.

Post-grad literature discipline would enhance my knowledge of the grand writers of the English-speaking world and give me further opportunity to evaluate my gifts and determine (or modify) my vocational goals.

If pornography tempts me, I will refuse obscene pictures lest my imagination run away with itself and plunge me into evil behavior and despair.

So my upbringing was contaminated with talking behind backs; as an adult, I refuse to contaminate the reputations of other people.

Though I listened to complainers in my formative years I will not imitate anything so bad. To the contrary, I will put the spirit of construction, not destruction, into my lifestyle.

**Action—Bringing Imagination to Fruition.** In the late 1940s Jerome, a newspaper journalist, found Christ and dreamed of becoming a clergyman. He heard of the divinity school at New College, Edinburgh University, with its famous professors, John Baillie and James S. Stewart. Could he afford such an adventure? He would seek God's will. The divine answer, "Yes," spurred him onto making plans. The plans turned into sailing to England and from there taking the train to Edinburgh.

Once ensconced in the theology school, he chose a mentor and together they selected a thesis topic. Then he researched day by day in the libraries of Edinburgh—the world-renowned New College library, the excellent public library, and the United Kingdom's copyright library. Faithful and persistent work, data discovery, drafts, massaging the drafts, consultations with his advisor—all of it came to flower in an acceptable thesis and the doctorate from one of the world's foremost institutions of learning.

This highly creative endeavor so absorbed Jerome that he quite forgot the mind-worrying, gone-by days, the sleepless nights, the wear and tear of a job he did not feel called to, the threat to his well-being. Imagination, now seen as the gift of God, had brought a whole new sense of life—abundant, free, meaningful, and fulfilling.

### *Rekindled? Yes!*

# Day 5:
## EXPECT THE UNEXPECTED

### *Rx info-med*

Novelists create. But they do not know where their creativity will go. The plotline may take a quite different pathway than expected; characters will say and do things unanticipated. Authors' pens surprise even, perhaps especially, the writers themselves.

This common writer experience is a metaphor of what happens in any creative endeavor. Alexander Fleming discovered the first antibiotic, penicillin, quite by accident in 1928. By chance he noticed a strange mold related to staphylococci. To his astonishment, he found the penicillin had remarkable antibiotic powers. Playing with cultures, a fulfilling, though sometimes agonizing creative activity, he made a totally unexpected discovery. This surprising new mold ate bacteria!

My first teaching assignment came at Seattle Pacific University, where a physicist, C. Hoyt Watson, served as president. He loved playing with ideas. On plane or train, he would take an administrative challenge, mull it over in his head, and come up with a solution not everyone, perhaps no one else, would have thought of. In a committee assigned to work with the architect for a new music hall on campus, I watched President Watson quiz the designer. One question sticks in my mind: could the blueprint call for a new way of disposing trash? The architect listened. Dr. Watson, on the spot, verbally drew a disposal plan unique and remarkably workable. The architect, with a knowing look of satisfaction, said, "Yes, Mr. President, we can do that."

One can almost put words to a rule of creative thinking: The result will surprise you. Expect the unexpected, and if your imagination works along positive lines of thought, the solution to your problem will have merit, often more exciting than you could have anticipated.

***Rekindled? Yes!***

# Day 6
# EXPECT JOY

### Rx info-med

Imagine the excitement, the sheer thrill, of Sir Alexander Fleming when, after years of experimentation and the help of others (Howard Florey of Australia and Ernst Chain of Great Britain who showed how penicillin could be made ready for medical use in 1940), he saw his unexpected discovery used to cure disease. What joy indeed!

The life of exploration, innovation and discovery fills one with *joie de vivre*. Listen to a Mozart piano concerto with its racy fingering, tracing the emerging blueprint evolving in the composer's mind. Sense the delight, the sheer excitement. No wonder Karl Barth said Mozart's music was made in heaven. Eugene Peterson, famous for his books and paraphrase of the Bible, *The Message,* says, "I think it's interesting that Karl Barth, the theologian who has influenced me most, was mostly influenced by Mozart. Mozart was a theme in his life. I think he learned a lot about writing theology by listening to Mozart" ("Interview" 18).

No one can read very far in a Peterson book without sensing something of the same joy one hears in a Mozart symphony. And that deep happiness you will find in many theologians. The enormously creative Thomas Aquinas commented, "Joy is the noblest human act."

Teilhard de Chardin, an unusually imaginative theologian, said, "Joy is the most infallible sign of the presence of God." Compare that jubilant statement with another Karl Barth sentence: "Laughter is the closest thing to God's grace" (see James Martin 15).

And what creator does not cry joy when reflecting on the Creator's world? Ralph Waldo Emerson captured this joyous spirit when he penned a quick sentence rich in imagination: "Earth laughs in flowers." Teresa of Avila, that delightful saint who seemed never weary of exploring the spiritual life, pled, "From somber devotions and sour-faced saints, good Lord, deliver us." (This famous statement of heart joy, though typical of St. Teresa's spirit, cannot be documented in her works. See  Martin 69.) What absorbed researcher, gathering data and couching it in inviting and ordered language, doesn't find rich satisfaction and genuine delight in discovery and design?

Creativity come full circle breeds something akin to a "seventh heaven" experience and puts burnout in a corner.

***Rekindled? Yes!***

# Day 7
## HEALTHY PRIDE

### *Rx info-med*

Three vignettes.

Our family, driving in scenic Holland, spotted a Nether-lands windmill home, complete with all the Dutch accou-terments. At the invitation of the man of the house, we went in, saw the mother and her little children, wife and little girl wearing long skirts, small boys in bulging pan-taloons, and all feet shod in wooden shoes. The interior with its hanging copper pans and Delft fireplace decora-tions, as charming as the exterior with its huge wind-blown propellers, left an indelible impression on our brains. Upon leaving, our preteen daughter Cherith said, "That man was so proud of his house." His smile tele-graphed exactly that.

I love watching the *Antiques Road Show*. Last night the highlight, an Art Deco bracelet, captured my attention with unusual fascination. The daughter who brought it to the show explained that her father, years before, ordered the piece of jewelry for her mother. Remarkable images appeared on the wide bracelet—for example a woman pushing a baby buggy with wheels that moved at the touch of a finger. The craftsman had shaped each of the several images surrounding the circlet with diamonds and precious stones. Would you believe that husband could find a jeweler to create so unusual a wrist band? What pride that craftsman must have felt upon making the bracelet, then handing it to the proud husband to present to his wife!

Vignette number three: Our grandson Christopher suffers from cystic fibrosis. With his debilitating disease comes a myriad of complications—breathing challenges, cardiac issues, depression, etc. Christopher can do little, but I notice that when he conceives of a doable project, then actually executes it, he's joyfully fulfilled. For example, he loves building winter fires for Kathleen and me. The family room glows with warmth, and he joins in the delight, sometimes sitting by the fire with his grandparents.

Two days ago a friend went with Christopher to a farm to fill his pickup truck with firewood, which he delivered in our driveway. Yesterday he brought tools, including a power saw, cut the timber into logs, then stacked them neatly in the garage woodbin. No one could observe Christopher and miss his pride in accomplishment. Medicine indeed for his spirit.

***Rekindled? Yes!***

***        ***                    ***

## WEEK'S SUMMARY POINT OF
## HOPE AND HEALING

**Creative output opens the windows of my soul to restoration.**

# WEEK 7

# REKINDLED: RADICAL SELF-GIVING LOVE

Where there is great love there is always miracles.

—Willa Cather

We can do no great things—only small things with great love.

—Mother Teresa

# Day 1

## DEFINING LOVE

*Rx info-med*

In our culture we use the word *love* in a variety of ways. A woman sees a pretty sweater in a department store window and comments, "I just love that garment." She enters the store and buys it. We sign a letter, "Lots of love," and mean it with some degree of sincerity. A woman looks up to "my gorgeous husband" and says, "I love him." We speak of loving a friend or a lovable place (the name Philadelphia comes from two Greek words meaning "the city of the loving [friendly] brethren"). Toyohiko Kagawa, the famous Christian evangelist of Japan, loved God with all his heart and demonstrated that affectionate dedication by living in the slums of Kobe to identify with and help the people in that atrocious setting. Mother Teresa said a lot about love and demonstrated it with a lifetime of unparalleled service, especially to those imprisoned in poverty. All these expressions of love, and more, signal the human desire to love and be loved. We are made for love.

Often we speak of three Greek words for love: *eros, philia,* and *agape.* You may have seen these terms in your Sunday School or Bible study materials. Perhaps Greek is better than English at describing love by using words with greater specificity and precision. *Eros* is a kind of stimulus-response attraction or passion that says if I give my office-partner Bill a Christmas present, I may get one in return. This kind of behavior borders on manipulation and sometimes does indeed become just that. *Eros* more frequently refers to a kind of glandular and emotional response in sexual experience. Often the Greeks thought of beauty as setting the mind on fire with passion.

Certainly love as friendship (*philia*) plays its role. The New Testament refers to love primarily as *agape* and sometimes *philia*. In pre-biblical Greek, *agape* and *philia* could take on a number of meanings, but in the New Testament the sacrificial love of Jesus for His enemies kicks *love* into a far higher orbit. Jesus' call for love requires forsaking all to follow God. It prompted the Good Samaritan to show kindness beyond the requirements of the law. This radical self-giving made Jesus choose to go to the cross.

Jesus' distinctive love relates to losing your life to find it. Just there lies a major therapy for burnout, which explains the fulfillment in the life of Donna, who seems never to stop giving herself. She loves little children, worked many years in her local day care center and now watches small ones in her home. For years she took care of her husband, who became quite debilitated from a stroke. She loved caregiving, though no doubt she found it terribly trying at times. After Bob died, she said, "I told the Lord He had taken my love and also my job," and chuckled with delight as she reflected on the joyous long years she attended her husband.

God graced Donna as she gave herself unstintingly to her lifelong companion.

### *Rekindled? Yes!*

# Day 2

## IN-DEPTH THERAPY: "LOVING GOD"—JESUS' SUMMARY OF THE LAW (I)

### *Rx info-med*

Eugene Peterson's rendering of Mark 12:28-34 puts fresh light on a central message of our Lord:

> One of the religion scholars came up. Hearing the lively exchanges of question and answer and seeing how sharp Jesus was in his answers, he put in his question: "Which is most important of all the commandments?"

> Jesus said, "The first in importance is, 'Listen, Israel: The Lord your God is one, so love the Lord God with all your passion and prayer and intelligence and energy.' And here is the second: 'Love others as well as you love yourself.' There is no other commandment that ranks with these."

> The religion scholar said, "A wonderful answer, Teacher! So lucid and accurate—that God is one and there is no other. And loving him with all passion and intelligence and energy, and loving others as well as you love yourself. Why, that's better than all offerings and sacrifices put together!"

> When Jesus realized how insightful he was, he said, "You're almost there, right on the border of God's kingdom."

> After that, no one else dared ask a question.

Jesus' answer to the scholar came as a surprise. It still comes as a surprise to men and women today. Loving God, others, and self—that's the sum total of the law? Well, yes. And that His audience felt compelled to ponder that simple but profound statement of the truth explains the total silence.

How do you process Jesus' threefold declaration? Something like the following?

> To worship more than one god—money, power, reputation, whatever—fractures belief, possesses schizophrenic power, and can tear me apart. With multiple gods, greed breaks through moral parameters, then my conscience troubles me. And that burned-out feeling makes its presence felt.

So where, really, is my security? Not in the three classic sin categories–power, sex and money. Not in home, health, or reputation. True, God uses all these to grace me with His security, but in themselves they can offer only passing safety and stability. If all these run out, God's love never, but never, leaves the believing heart. Thus, the famous Lamentations 3 passage, from which Thomas Chisholm got his inspiration for writing the well-known Gospel hymn, "Great is Thy Faithfulness." Eugene Peterson's paraphrase of the Lamentations verses (22-24) makes wonderfully vivid God's love, His protective love:

> God's loyal love couldn't have run out,
> His merciful love couldn't have dried up.
> They're created new every morning.
> How great your faithfulness!
> I'm sticking with GOD (I say it over and over).
> He's all I've got left.

## *Rekindled? Yes!*

# Day 3

# IN-DEPTH THERAPY: "LOVING OTHERS"—

# JESUS' SUMMARY OF THE LAW (2)

### *Rx info-med*

To love God with one's whole being and lifestyle–that is primary and makes possible the other two components, love of neighbor and love of self.

A self-preoccupied woman, housed in a senior citizens home, complained of emotional disturbance. Her psychiatrist prescribed therapy in a significant word: OTHERS–focus not on yourself but OTHERS.

Stanley Jones created a therapeutic image for anyone who felt threatened by a *nervous breakdown*. "Go to the other side of the tracks," counseled Brother Stanley, "and find someone in need." Healthy people find a need and fill it.

Dr. Jones said more. In his listing of "The Twelve Apostles of Ill Health," he cited self-preoccupation as one of the culprits. Precisely there he put his finger, by implication, on something crucial. Auntie Corser, one of the healthiest Christians I knew in my growing-up years, always seemed to me a very happy soul. She would call mother to say, "Grace, send Donald running. I have just brought a breakfast cake out of the oven and it's for your family." Believe me, I went running! The smell of her baked goods, the even better taste at our breakfast table, the glow of her giving smile so captured my soul that I cannot forget it 75 years later. Auntie Corser was the picture of well-being.

### *Rekindled? Yes!*

# Day 4

# IN-DEPTH THERAPY:

# "LOVING YOURSELF"—

# JESUS' SUMMARY OF THE LAW (3)

### *Rx info-med*

Now we come to love of oneself, self-esteem. Mother Teresa observes that if we love ourselves we can love others. So true, for we are projective creatures. People who do not respect themselves project their self-dislike, often self-hatred, on others.

In the classroom we put a Power Point on the screen that reads *Imago Dei*, meaning God made us in His image. If God created us, He respects us. What potter dislikes his creation?

Still we doubt ourselves. Self-doubt, the product of original sin, requires overcoming grace. Initial conversion helps, and this experience explains in part why newborn Christians possess joy. For many, however, feelings of inadequacy persist. Sometimes new awareness of our limitations emerges, for the Sprit reveals us to ourselves—our faults as well as our gifts. To know we have growing edges and that God Himself stands ready to help us improve is a normal step in ongoing maturation, in appropriate self-love. Sincere Christians welcome self-revelation because the more dependent we become on the Lord, the more He can do for and with us.

For many, especially introverts, growth in self-esteem is a lifelong process, the process we call sanctification. The closer we grow to the Creator, the nearer we come to the *Imago Dei.*

Spiritual direction, which takes many forms, is of major help. We grow in fellowship, what the New Testament calls *koinonia.* In community we learn more and more to love God, self, and, therefore, others. You will want to list the sources of spiritual direction. Here's an example:

*Finding a Spiritual Director.* Locate someone spiritually mature and characterized by wisdom. Often a director has had training in the art of spiritual guidance.

*Getting into a Bible-believing church, one with a good self-image.* Self-esteem is contagious. An institution that respects itself goes a long way toward creating people who honor themselves with humility and Godlike love.

*Finding a sharing group.* Small groups characterized by honesty and respect for each member can provide enormous guidance for growing to be like Jesus. Confidentiality marks healthy disciple groups, for we need an open atmosphere enabling us to share anything: confession, ideas, theories, insights, discoveries.

*Having conjugal direction.* A spiritually tuned spouse can provide support, correction, and information in the context of intimacy. Often wives become first-rate spiritual directors because of the female nurturing instinct, and they have a special gift for instilling love and encouragement. Often the male, with his eye on outcomes, provides uplift, encouragement and motivation. The bottom line is that males and females need each other.

How many more spiritual formation possibilities can you list? Christian books, private and congregational worship, retreats, Sunday school, or singing the grand hymns of the Church with their rich spiritual/theological content (e.g., the hymns of Charles Wesley, saturated with the message of sacrificial love). This list does indeed go on.

Expose yourself to Bible-based spiritual direction in any of the forms God directs, and watch your self-esteem grow and burnout disintegrate.

### *Rekindled? Yes!*

# Day 5
# THE ANCIENT PRAYER OF *EXAMEN*

## *Rx info-max*

Ignatius of Loyola developed what was to become a classic prayer pattern called *examen*. The term comes from a kind of Church Latin meaning to put into balance, to examine consciousness and conscience. As to the first, one thinks of how God has been present. The second implies asking God for correction and improvement, not an exercise, by the way, in morbid introspection. (For more on St. Ignatius, see Foster and Smith, 33-39; Lonsdale 99-100.)

Nothing lifts one's sense of self-esteem more than reflecting on the many ways God presents Himself to us, loves us. God loves me enough to lead and provide. In this part of the prayer of *examen* you may want to list the good things grace has brought you. (In my own prayer life, I list the pluses morning and evening, making this part of the *examen* experience a daily affair. I get specific: a friend took me to lunch, I had money to pay for car repairs, teatime today filled with jovial talk and stimulating information.)

The *examen* prayer, then, relates not only to tracing the finger of God on mercies and positive expressions of love; it also calls for hearing Him indicate my growing edges. Openness to where I fall short of the holy life–in thought, word or deed–means I want to change and become more like Christ. As those changes become reality, my self-esteem develops a step further, and nothing lifts self-image, appropriate self-love, so much as becoming more like Jesus.

### *Rekindled? Yes!*

# Day 6

# GOING DEEPER WITH A KICK-OFF SUGGESTION BY THOMAS MERTON

### Rx info-med

This business of self-esteem, appropriate self-love, is a sticky wicket, so we must go deeper. Thomas Merton makes a declaration that helps us. This monk and writer believed an important step toward sanctity is self-knowledge. Let's go deeply enough in prayer and thought to cut through the layers of egotism until we arrive at the center of ourselves where God Himself lives.

How do we implement Brother Merton's guidance? To begin to trace his answer, read his fascinating autobiography *The Seven Storey Mountain,* and add to it Foster and Smith's *Devotional Classics,* the chapter on Merton.

Let me answer the implementation question by some of my own practical suggestions. Begin with stripping away fleeting ego concerns that provide only momentary self-respect to discover the real self and the God within. Herein lies a fundamental concern.

We must ask God for *courage.* Request the Almighty to help us work through the natural hesitancy about self-exploration, the fear of what we may discover. This reluctance explains why we erect elaborate coverings and defenses against self-discovery. Only God Himself can give us grace to explore, and sometimes we need a spiritual director to help us. Seminaries provide directors, soul friends, advisors to assist men and women over the hurdles of self-finding. By this constructive method today's pastors train to become spiritual directors to their parishioners. For both pastor and people, the process of looking within takes courage.

Second, see your *social relationships* as a mirror. We cannot, by raw self-confrontation, really see ourselves. Somebody observed that it's "as hard to see oneself as to look backwards without turning around." Introspection in isolation yields few results. To jump over this hurdle, look at the word *saints.* It never appears in the singular in the New Testament. Saints know themselves and the God in them. We learn about ourselves from others—their body language, tone, acceptance and support.

Finally, *serve others* in the spirit of glad and eager sharing. Mother Teresa found God in Calcutta while serving the poorest of the poor and, in the process, discovered herself and the God within. She found the meaning of her life and therefore the self-respect, the self-love, required for doing God's assigned task with confidence.

Apply Merton's admonition to self-discovery as the Spirit guides you and remind yourself that the process takes time and patience. But the peace that emerges with growing insight, equilibrium in the presence of others, and in-depth serenity, brings confidence that frees one to live with abandonment and contentment.

### Rekindled? Yes!

# Day 7

# A MAJOR CLUE: REMEMBERING

### *Rx info-med*

"We live by our memories," goes the time-honored proverb, and it reveals a profound biblical secret. In both Old
and New Testaments, the word *remember* occurs over
and over. Psalmists remember Israel's victories. Jesus
admonishes us to celebrate His supper "in remembrance
of Me" (1 Cor. 11:24-25). Scripture reveals the power of
the God who acts, who never fails His people. Note the
repeated story of Israel as in Deuteronomy, the books of
Kings, and Samuel, and the place of Jesus in the Jewish
world recounted in Peter's sermon at Pentecost (Acts 2).
By example, then, the Bible leads us to the renewal of
faith and love by recalling the turning points in our own
experiences of blessing and rescue, documentations of
God's unremitting love.

In remembering God signals a central and very hearten-
ing message: He cares for you because you are important.
You are one of God's children. That truth penetrates our
hearts and lets us know that God is the Control Agent of
our lives, which gives us cause enough to love God su-
premely.

In which trajectories do your memories move? Into the
black recesses of your Hiroshimas or Vietnams, or, con-
trariwise, into remembrances bright with moon landings

and smart phones? Decide to live by memories that inspire great possibilities. Psychologists say that remembering brings many positive results. Edward Hoffman shows that "science has discovered that nostalgia itself is good for us" (24-33).

God calls us to see our present circumstances in the light of His loving acts in the past. Peterson's rendition of the outset of Psalm 103 underscores this poignant truth:

> O my soul, bless God.
> From head to toe, I'll bless his holy name!
> O my soul, bless God,
> Don't forget a single blessing!" (vv. 1-2, MSG)

Read the rest of that great psalm to remind you what God has done and note the specifics that remind us of His love:

> [He] forgives your sins,…
> heals your diseases,…
> redeems you from hell,…
> crowns you with love and mercy,…
> wraps you in goodness… (vv. 3-5).

The psalmist even goes on to declare that God puts everything right, followed by another listing of God's loving mercies.

Forgetting all these *agape/philia* mercies so debilitates the soul that, losing heart, we wander from God and we behave in ways that spoil our God-desired image of ourselves. A vivid example is found in the book of Judges where God declares that the Israelites did evil because they "forgot the Lord their God and served the Baals and the Asherahs" (Judges 3:7). God intended this prod to remembrance to encourage His people in loving relationship with Him and their fellow Israelites. Want to lose legitimate, God-given pride in yourself? Forget. Just forget all He has done to cement your sense of relationship with God and yourself.

The Bible's call for double love, for God and His people, comes to focus in all the memorials: personal remembrances (Jer. 15:15), memorials (Matt. 26:13), corporate recollections (Deut. 5:15; Josh. 4:4-24). Note how the Passover (Exod. 12:14) and the Lord's Supper (Luke 22:19; 1 Cor. 11:24-26) bring to mind God's work of deliverance, rescue, and salvation. Observe, too, the memorial stones in the Old Testament (Exod. 28:12; Josh. 4:4-24).

God's admonition to recall His law  reminds us that the Law serves us and is a loving set of rules to help, not hinder  (e.g., notably Neh. 9:16-18). Do a careful reading of Psalm 77 and see how the writer moves from doubt to deliverance which is reason enough to know God's unfaltering love.

The Bible relates the role of remembering as a means of announcing that God loves us and desires with His total being that we love Him back.

### *Rekindled? Yes!*

\*\*\*             \*\*\*             \*\*\*

## WEEK'S SUMMARY POINT OF
## HOPE AND HEALING

**Jesus said, "'Love the Lord your God with all your passion and prayer and intelligence.'" This is the most important, the first on any list. But there is a second to set alongside it: "'Love others as well as you love yourself.'" These two commands are pegs; everything in God's Law and the Prophets hangs from them (Matt. 22:37-40, MSG).**

# WEEK 8

# REKINDLED: BRAIN, BODY, AND BRAWN

Look to your health; and if you have it, praise God,
and value it next to a good conscience;
for health is the second blessing
that we mortals are capable of;
a blessing that money cannot buy.

—Izaak Walton
*Compleat Angler*


There are two places I've never heard
of a man having a nervous breakdown.
One is in a swimming pool
while he's stretching his muscles;
the other is in front of a fireplace
while he's stretching his soul."

—Rear Admiral Lamont Pugh
Surgeon General of the U.S. Navy

# Day 1

# THREE BASIC THERAPIES FOR

# WELL-BEING

### *Rx info-med*

Research data in exercise physiology, stress, brain, and spirituality provide us with three strategic therapies that overlap and interweave with each other.

*Deep relaxation* provides opportunity for body, soul, and brain to enter a whole new and fresh world. Perfect quiet initiates restoration. How well the Psalmist knew the restorative powers of relaxation and rest! Psalm 116:7-8, for example, gathers up the refreshment that results from living in the tranquil presence of God:

> I said to myself, "Relax and rest.
> God has showered you with blessings.
> Soul, you've been rescued from death;
> Eye, you've been rescued from tears;
> And you, Foot, were kept from stumbling (MSG).

Private and corporate worship are God's vehicles for bringing to the soul, that is the total person (*nephesh*), deep calm. Peace is the therapy sensed in the hearts of true worshippers upon leaving the prayer room or the house of God.

God-established serenity, now quietly present in the sub-conscious, comes to conscious awareness on the way home from work at a stop sign or on entering an active home after a hard day's labor, and calms the spirit for sound sleep at the close of the day.

Here's a quick word about sleep: Researchers today believe a major function of sleep relates to the brain processing the day's exposures. The brain, scientists discovered, never stops working. This while-you-sleep brain operation turns out to be profound therapy.

*Physical exercise* assists the relaxation process. A good swim may well prepare one for a restful night. We have also learned that the brain operates better with physical exercise. Fatigue toxins drain away in vigorous exercise, reducing stress and initiating bodily repose. Body tone enhances and strengthens emotional and biologic defenses against mental and physiologic diseases. The heart muscle profits from appropriate exercise and arteries stay cleaner. Every person would do well to consult his or her doctor about a workable exercise program.

*Adequate diet* relates to the frustrating challenges that can easily result in distress. When artery walls thicken with cholesterol, demands on the heart and circulatory system increase. Fruits, vegetables, and plenty of water do the body, and therefore the emotional system, immense good. To the contrary, fat, sugar, and salt in overabundance often result in sluggishness to both body and brain. Since "we are the temple of the living God" (2 Cor. 7:16), the spiritual life can suffer as a result of careless intake.

One wonders how much depression, both emotional and spiritual, issues from eating too much and consuming the wrong kinds of foods. A frank look at results may spur one onto disciplined diet. Then watch respiration regenerate, arthritis pain reduce, even vision improve.

We have then, three missiles—relaxation, exercise, and diet—forming a triad of weaponry, tested by research and experience, opening the door to wholeness and freedom from burnout. More on fitness as week eight unfolds.

In the meantime, here's a thought-provoking comment by my rehabilitation physician granddaughter Kathleen: "If people would exercise, drink enough water, and eat right, doctors would be out of a job." Yes, of course this statement is an exaggeration but closer to the truth than we often think.

***Rekindled? Yes!***

# Day 2

## THE POWER OF VISION

*Rx info-med*

Neuroscientist David Eagleman, in his book *Incognito: The Secret Lives of the Brain,* announces his surprising research finding: "About one-third of the human brain is devoted to vision." He cites experiments with people who lose their sight. When they can no longer see, they continue visioning in pictures. In place of eyes that see, "[v]isual-tactile substitution glasses can take the visual input from a camera and translate it into vibrations on a pad on the person's back." Give the patient a week and the pressure on the back becomes the vehicle for instituting the new way of seeing. Eagleman says we see not so much with our eyes as with our brains.

The massive bits and pieces lodged in the gray matter run our lives. We drive without pondering each move, just as we swim unconsciously aware of every stroke. What establishes unconscious patterns of behavior is determined by what we inherit, learn, and absorb. We have, tucked away in our minds, lots of material for picture-making (see Moll's response to *Incognito* with Eagleman quotations, 19).

So we *see* the temptation (the illustration in Moll is chocolate cake vs. health concerns) and refuse to yield. The trap opens wide if we yield, and if caught in the

same repeated behavior, it becomes part of the unconscious driving force of the personality. *There's that cake
again. Have a piece, maybe two pieces.*

John Medina, Director of the Brain Center for Applied
Learning Research at Seattle Pacific University and Professor of Bioengineering in the University of Washington
School of Medicine, observes that we must, in learning
something, "repeat to remember" and "remember to repeat" (Medina 95ff, 120ff).

What do we want to remember? Put personally and specifically, what do I want to vision, to settle in my mind as
expressive of my lifestyle? I have a choice. Shall I put
into my mind negative or positive pictures? Shall I repeat
the gossip or the good I've learned about Joe at the office? Will I underscore the slight of the boss at Christmas
or remember the birthday gift he so graciously and sur-
prisingly presented to me in August? And when I ponder
something so important as professional or vocational
goals, do I decide to reinforce lesser or greater goals, or
perhaps both (e.g., keeping a cleaner desk and serving
more people in a managerial position)?

Recently I read the account of a Jesuit priest born with
one arm. Interested in athletic activity, he decided on a
great goal: to help physically challenged people get into
sports. One day, evidently in the gym, a man who had
broken his arm complained, "Father, you cannot imagine
what's it's like not to be able to lift your right arm." A
sophisticated name for that kind of self-absorption is *sol-
ipsism*, the product of negative and introverted thinking.
The priest knew exhilaration, the joyful enthusiasm, of

helping people with his overcomer state of mind. One wonders if the man with the broken arm enjoyed calling attention to himself more than getting well.

Wise people see themselves with a broken arm empathizing with people worse off than themselves. They also refuse self-sympathy and picture themselves mended and whole again.

### *Rekindled? Yes!*

# Day 3

# INTER-PERSONAL RELATIONSHIPS:

# THE BIG CHALLENGE

### *Rx info-med*

Medina's research shows the enormous power of the brain for solving problems, especially meeting interpersonal challenges. This overcoming propensity of the human brain explains, he says, our survival in the long journey of the human race.

My wife, Kathleen, and I enjoy our friend Shirley who comes to tea on Sunday afternoons. While most of the conversation fills with the pleasantries of life, including our relationship to God, sometimes it turns on our interconnection with fellow human beings. In those moments, Shirley talks about her office boss who is critical and unreasonable. Our tea guest asks repeatedly, "How can I get along with Connie? Sometimes I want to resign my job."

Shirley faces a problem we all confront at one time or another—personality differences, often, as in Shirley's case, radical differences. The neuroscientists tell us that every brain is individualized, that the wiring is more complex than the web. We live and work with very difficult personalities, at times just plain unaccommodating. In the case of Shirley, her speech and ideation pattern come across, almost immediately, as bright, creative, and social. Connie, in possession of a quite different set of gifts, finds Shirley difficult to supervise. Shirley, knowing she cannot escape Connie, wisely searches for ways to play on the team. And she will in all probability succeed and, in the process, learn another coping skill.

One of the happy grandmother-and-grandchild stories in current circulation instructs us all in interpersonal relatedness. At lunch in a restaurant, little Tyler says table grace something like this: "O Lord, thank you for the food and my granny, and please tell her lunch can be even better if she gets me ice cream." A woman, sitting at a nearby table, talks in a voice loud enough for everyone around to hear: "That's a terrible prayer. What are parents teaching their kids today? Disgusting!" With this comment, the little fellow nearly bursts into tears and asks, "Grandma, did I do it wrong?" Just then a nice man puts his arm around Tyler and says, "That was a great prayer." "Really?" the small boy asks as he looks up into the eyes of the kind gentleman. "Yes," he says. "I'm positive. Ice cream is good for the soul."

Grandma orders a dish of ice cream, complete with a red cherry on the top. But the little guy does not eat his dessert. Picking up his plate, he takes it to the ugly-spirited woman, puts it on the table in front of her and says, "Ice cream is good for the soul, and your soul needs it."

The loving kindness of a little boy penetrated the soul of a cranky woman.

**_Rekindled? Yes!_**

# Day 4
# EXERCISE DOES MORE
# THAN YOU THINK

### *Rx info-med*

What surprised me when I started doing research on the human brain was the relation of physical activity to brain health. Of Medina's 12 brain rules, exercise comes first. His research indicates that physical exercise boosts brain power. More, the data tell us that exercise is a predictor of longevity, is used in treating brain disorders, enhances cognitive efficiency, and radically reduces the chance of dementia. More, exercise is fun. Dr. Medina calls it "cognitive candy" (*Brain Rules*).

Psychiatrist Gary Small, MD, directs the UCLA Longevity Center. His findings suggest that exercise prevents Alzheimer's (*The Alzheimer's Prevention Program*). In fact, he, like Medina, lists exercise first, this time as it relates specifically to Alzheimer's. "You can build brain muscle," Dr. Small observes. He goes on to say one does not have to turn into a big athlete. Just do things like parking your car at a distance to force yourself to walk or climb stairs rather than use the elevator ("*Protect Yoursel...,*" 39-40). The article also promotes eating well and cites research indicating that being overweight doubles the risk for dementia, and obesity quadruples it.)

American astronauts enhanced their stair climbing by doing two at a time. If one caught another climbing one step at a time, he or she was fined! Lung health moderates stress by reducing breathlessness, pounding pulse and lightheadedness.

Exercise also helps keep weight down. Each additional pound of fat means more work for the heart, and, in the event of surgery, makes the doctor cut through more flesh. The tricky fact about weight is that for many people it seems to have mystical powers to multiply. An average of two pounds added yearly can mean twenty excess pounds in ten years, forty in twenty, eighty in forty years. Heaviness sneaks up on us without dietary and workout disciplines.

Dr. Laurence E. Morehouse served as Director of the Human Performance Laboratory, University of California, Los Angeles. He observed that in men and women with pulse rates over 92, the mortality rate jumped to four times greater than in people with rates of 67 or less. This piece of data reminds me of my faculty friend at Greenville College in Illinois who ran regularly and thereby reduced his heart rate to well below the male average of 72-76.

One of the interesting and common side effects of running is addiction to the exercise. Such practice may have its ill effects, but how much better to be habituated to exercise than, say, to tobacco, alcohol, or prescription drugs! Half a pack of cigarettes a day, says one researcher, ups the risk of death from heart attack by some 60 percent, while a full pack daily lifts the risk to 110 percent. Yes, we argue about the 90-year-old who smoked a pipe or enjoyed cigars, but such instances appear more anecdotal than scientific. What is scientific relates to studies showing that even nonsmokers in a smoking environment—called second-hand smoke—can, and often do, contract cancer.

The famous cardiac researcher, Paul Dudley White, observed that firm thighs mean a good heart, and he made it his practice to examine thigh tone before doing surgery. Walking helps to strengthen legs, as does running.

Some authorities recommend swimming as the best exercise, especially if one has a tendency to lose joint health by running. Whatever your choice of exercise, know that keeping fit and maintaining normal weight, can reward you with enormous benefits:

*Depression can be reduced, even cleared. Not everyone, but some modify or eliminate depression by a workout program. The following data, in a recent *Los Angeles Times* report, helps us put this benefit into perspective. In the report we learn that eleven per cent of Americans as early as 12 years of age take antidepressants. Antidepressants are the most common prescription drugs for those aged 18-44. Nearly a fourth of women 40-59 take antidepressants. Consumption of such medications increased by 400 per cent from 1988-2008 (*"11%"* C10.)

*Surgery is far less dangerous due to greater pulmonary reserve, lower incidence of anesthetic complications, and less fat tissue for the surgeon to contend with.

*When one goes for an annual checkup, the doctor experiences less difficulty in abdominal examination (to locate organ enlargement, tumors, etc.).

*Psychological rewards include the sense of well-being.

*Physical energy enhances with lifting weights, swimming, cycling, walking, whatever.

Here are two stories, the one a warning, the other a victory.

Nathan did not have time to attend to fitness. He died in his fifties, having given little attention to exercise, diet, and his unconquered tobacco habit. Because his arteries were clogged, surgery succeeded in extending his life only a few months.

Now the good news account. David knew that the price of vitality is discipline. One cardiac attack after another could not deter his determination to get well. Slowly, surely he developed his body by jogging and diet, strengthened his mind by reading, and organized an enormous set of observations about life and Scripture into a vast and eminently useful filing system. He grew closer to God by prayer and meditation. Once his cardiac issues were under control, he lived a happy, productive, and very busy life as a teaching pastor.

For more on the power of exercise to keep us well, see "Exercise and Depression" on the Web, an article first published in the "Special Health Report from Harvard Medical School, 'Understanding Depression,'" a great resource for further information. In the one-page Web article, "Exercise and Depression," the role of consistent exercise, researchers discovered, plays a pretty major part in treating depression. It also helps in lowering blood pressure, protecting one from cancer and cardiac threats, and boosting self-esteem.

### *Rekindled? Yes!*

# Day 5

# COURAGE LEADS TO SPIRITUAL AND

# EMOTIONAL BRAWN

***Rx info-med***

This working and therapeutic principle is explained best in the following examples.

No one lives through this life free of roadblocks. Some of these challenges come across as formidable indeed. Like the student born with dwarfism. The college community watched as she made her way across campus, worked through the rows to her seat in morning chapel, slid into place in the classroom. What impressed all of us on the faculty and in the student body was her cheery style. She even made fun of herself in public. One day she honked at me as she drove through town. She waved and smiled big as life. If I remember correctly, she studied to become a teacher, and you can believe that when she called for order in the classroom, she got it! "Don't mess with Alice" came through loud and clear. She had developed courage.

Mother Teresa sat with her leader nuns for an administrative meeting. The chairperson introduced "a problem." In your imagination, hear Mother, with her firm and projective tone, reordering the mood of the committee: "Not a problem but a gift!" She knew full well that challenges are opportunities. Opportunities translate something bad into something good taking courage, brawn.

Beethoven, upon learning he would go deaf, cried, "I will blunt the sword of Fate." Well, he did! Such symphonies! Such string quartets! Such piano sonatas! He even wrote musical comedy—*scherzo* is Italian for *joke*. Yes, despite his many tragedies, hearing loss not the only one, Beethoven composed musical jokes. Quite a lot of them, in fact. Attitude, comingled with determination, developed courage and brawn to make magnificent music the world can never forget.

The celebrated English missionary Henry Martyn worked for years laboring to complete the Bible in Persian. He went to the Shah, excited to show his work. The Shah and his helpers looked at the Bible but left one by one, including the Shah himself. Now note Martyn's verbalized response to what must have been a severe let-down: "I refuse to be disappointed." Who does not revere Martyn as one of the great pioneer missionaries, exemplar *par excellence,* whose influence God used to call many a person to missionary service?

Yes! God knows human beings grow by overcoming roadblocks, by building spiritual and emotional muscle.

One more example. Recently an old man's story came to a health news publication. He assumed, he confessed, that upon reaching older age, muscle development ceased. Youth could develop girth but not the elderly. Nonetheless, he determined to stay as fit as possible, to work out. Lo and behold! Muscle growth. Brawn in old age (Reynolds B12).

The thin-skinned and the faint-of-heart will not survive long in this rough, rugged, and competitive world. An exercise physiologist's research yielded a quite remarkable finding. For every mile one walks or runs, an hour is added to that life. In class I quoted the University of Kentucky professor who made this discovery, only to have an overweight student challenge it. So I wrote to Dr. Anderson for documentation. He sent me a sheaf of pages enough in number to make a respectable PhD thesis. This set of research pages I housed in my office and invited anyone in the course to come read the materials. The overweight student never came.

Have you noticed that skeptics and complainers respond defensively to the challenges of life? Those who see obstacles not as problems but as opportunities develop brawn.

***Rekindled? Yes!***

# Day 6

# A SUMMARY LOOK AT JOHN MEDINA'S 12 BRAIN HEALTH PRINCIPLES—THE FIRST SIX

*Rx info-med*

Note again the full title of Medina's book: *Brain Rules: 12 Principles for Surviving and Thriving at Work, Home, and School.* Our bioengineer author presents a comprehensive set of laws to help us cope as well as thrive. Schoolteachers, in this anti-authoritarian age, burn out often. Dr. Medina's research suggests changes teachers can make to create a better learning atmosphere. In fact, the basic principles apply to business and just about every vocation and life situation.

Now for the first six, listed with commentary in my own words.

1. **Exercise**. We can hardly over-emphasize this number one principle. Why? Exercise boosts brain power. Suffer from sluggish thinking? From fear of forgetting (*senior moments*)? From cognitive deficiency? From lack of creativity? John Medina, the developmental molecular biologist, brings fresh encouragement and new hope by recommending this "cognitive candy" called exercise. Our brains become more active while we are up and doing. So he suggests committee meetings on foot, answering the phone while walking, and oth-

er work while on the move. While the idea may be so different than our work and study habits, we can surely add more activity to our lifestyle pattern, and the exercise physiologists would want to add to Dr. Medina's suggestions—any exercise at all. Exercise is indeed fun ("cognitive candy"), especially after habituating yourself to it.

2. **Survival**. The human capacity for solving problems and confronting challenges can only astonish the observant person. Chief among humankind's problems is interpersonal relations. Our capacity to understand each other takes a remarkable number of creative turns, some workable, others momentarily feasible, still others trash. God wires our brains to try, try, and try again. Manipulation, a questionable attempt, can create ill feelings especially when tried on perceptive persons. Yet, a box of chocolates, given in the right spirit, can bring to birth wholesome and productive relationships. The Bible gives many examples of solving interpersonal problems (e.g., Joseph and his brothers). The bottom line is to love others, even your enemies. Love opens the door to negotiation and a working team spirit.

3. **Wiring**. Every brain is wired differently. The wiring, vast as the highway system of America, goes in many directions, and experience adds additional wiring with many a fresh exposure. At any rate, we do well to recognize our very different personalities with varied ways of thinking and problem solving. The resulting possibilities for the cross-

fertilization of ideas, patiently lived with and pro-
cessed, possess power to create fresh ways of living and working.

4. **Attention**. Boredom robs us of that all-important
   brain function called attention. Enhanced attention
   creates an enlarged grasp of more items, even details. Emotion heightens attention, an indicator
   calling us to focus on right brain communication.
   (Daniel Goleman argued more than a decade ago
   that Emotional Quotient [EQ] matters more than
   IQ. *Emotional Intelligence* published in New York
   by Bantam Books, 1995.) For example, if one is
   caught in a rainstorm and puts up with wet clothes,
   one tends to remember that experience over
   against a more routine event.

   Medina moves to explain why human beings are
   not made to multitask. Today we hear a lot of talk
   about multitasking, especially relative to women,
   even arguing that the female brain lends itself to
   doing many things at once. Medina's research,
   however, concludes that human beings of either
   gender do their best work at focal-point. Multitasking produces negative results. Error goes up 50
   percent and work takes twice as long. Those who
   talk on their cell phones while driving take an
   enormous risk. Phone talk exacts the same lag in
   time response as alcohol, Dr. Medina says. Medina
   illustrates his concern by telling about the woman
   talking on her phone and running into a boy about
   to board a school bus, causing the lad serous brain

injury. She did not focus enough on her driving even to step on the brake pedal.

To ensure focus in work and study, people need to take rest periods to do well; otherwise, boredom and fatigue can set in.

5. **Short-term memory.** Medina tells us to "repeat to remember." The brain can hold information for 30 seconds; if repeated within 30 seconds, one keeps the data in mind for one or two hours.

6. **Long-term memory.** To remember over a period of time requires writing out and oral repetition. Interestingly, environment assists memory. If, for example, one experiences something in unusual circumstances—an auto accident or an especially gripping classroom experiment—memory sticks better.

*Rekindled? Yes!*

# Day 7
# JOHN MEDINA'S BRAIN RULES: SEVEN THROUGH TWELVE

*Rx info-med*

7. **Sleep**. Sleep well, think well–that's the rule in practical terms. We learn in sleep; the brain never stops working. In fact scientists think the real function of sleep lies in giving the brain time to process its exposures of the day. Sleep loss equals loss of mind function. Sleep takes up one-third of our lives. Repeated studies indicate that most Americans cheat themselves of sleep time. An interesting and telling NASA study reveals that a twenty-six-minute nap in the afternoon increases work efficiency by 34 percent. A forty-five minute nap keeps that efficiency boost going for more than six hours. One wonders how much burnout results from sheer lack of sleep.

   Research findings about sleep relate to both pain and efficiency. Lack of sleep exacerbates pain. Laws now appear on the books preventing doctors, for example, from working with little sleep. Who wants a surgeon, or any other professional, with foggy thinking, plus enhanced pain to add to the fog?

8. **Stress.** Stressed brains do not learn the same way as relaxed brains. When a kind of paralysis sets in due to perceived impossible solutions, resultant stress creates emotional instability. Some people, in an unreasonable and over-demanding atmosphere, go through what the researchers call "learned helplessness." (For more information Google "Learned Helplessness").

   Stress relates to fear and damages cognition, interrupts sleep, can cause depression, and even disturb the immune system, resulting in sickness. People threatened by burnout must take action—reconfiguring work and schedule, having a heart-to-heart talk with the boss, getting a new job—something to bring relief, thus allowing the brain to function normally and productively.

9. **Sensory integration.** When the senses work together, communication kicks in. In the preaching laboratory, I sometimes asked the technician to turn off sound so we could see the student preacher's playback only in body language. If the body does not articulate with the words spoken, communication lags. Add sound to the equation; if the tone does not articulate with intended meaning, once more communication lags. Sound and sight must work together.

   Starbucks works assiduously to keep the smell of coffee dominant. MacDonald's paints the inside of their stores with bright yellows to speed customers through lunch or dinner, thus making room for the next patrons. When senses work together, intended results emerge.

10. **Vision.** Vision trumps all other senses, says John Medina. God made our brains to do picture thinking. Brain research indicates that we do not see words in little letters but in tiny pictures. When *USA TODAY* started, experts said it would never succeed. In actual fact, it is the widest read newspaper in America. The reason? Pictures. Combine text with a good picture, and remembering goes up enormously (65 percent in one study). Even in PowerPoint, a better picture with less text produces greater communication impact.

11. **Gender.** For the last 20 years, we have been able to see brains with modern technological instruments. With improved brain mapping we now know women, for example, process quite differently than men, especially in details. The nurturing instinct of women combined with the male goal-driven linear instinct, brings together a much needed combination. Recognizing these differences in home and workplace can usher in a relaxed posture and recognition of the richer product when ladies and gentlemen, husbands and wives, work together.

12. **Exploration.** God made us natural and inveterate adventurers. We like to see and do new things. We want to learn how this experiment or that innovation will turn out. We relish discoveries. Employees spend 20 percent of their time at GOOGLE

free from assignments. As a result 50 percent of GOOGLE's innovations have come from the 20 percent free time. We are born curious, and with that curiosity comes brain development that never stops.

***Rekindled? Yes!***

\*\*\*          \*\*\*          \*\*\*

## WEEK'S SUMMARY POINT OF HOPE AND HEALING:

**Attention to brain and body function opens the door to liberated living.**

# WEEK 9

## REKINDLED: TIME

I was responsible for my own predicament.
*I* was the one who was saying yes
to every request for more work,
who kept taking on more writing projects,
and who refused to say no to any speaking gig,
no matter how busy I was.

—James Martin, S. J.
*From Heaven to Mirth*

## Day 1

## STEWARDSHIP OF TIME

*Rx info-med*

The research I conducted on fitness included a full spectrum of items: physical exercise, sleep, vacation, study, hobbies, devotional experience, sharing groups. My aim was to discern the level of fitness in the clergy. Research subjects included American whites and blacks, South African whites and blacks, ministers in England and Ireland, persons from many denominations, the moderately educated and those with advanced degrees, the old, young, and middle-aged.

I knew some lived carefully and productively; some even scheduled their days by the clock. Yet many a clergyperson subsisted with virtually no discipline of their time, which came as a shock to me. Even vacations and rest for renewal surfaced in the research sheets with notable uncertainty. I suspect a major reason lies in the often goal-conflicted nature of church work. Pastors labor in a context of such wide diversification that sometimes they suffer paralysis by not knowing just what to do. Frequent uncertainty about when and where to spend time complicates schedules even more. Still another dynamic relates to the pastor's availability—people often take advantage of their minister's time.

The mounting frustration accompanied with the lack of fulfillment easily results in burnout. My completed research indicates that clergyperson after clergyperson does not set aside adequate time for sermon preparation, prayer, Bible reading, family holidays, physical fitness and personal recreation. Feelings aroused by unproductiveness spell fatigue and discouragement. No wonder America loses hundreds of ministers each month (Demaray and Pickerill)! I saw on my returned survey sheets many attempts to cover up feelings of exaggerated guilt, posturing, and excuse-making.

An answer comes in prayerful decisions to correct the situation. Charlie W. Shedd's *Time for All Things* builds on the principle that time management is a theological matter. In other words, servants of God come face-to-face with a crucial spiritual challenge—managing our time with integrity. The Spirit of God calls all of us, whatever our vocation, to exercise personal gifts with disciplined tempo, while remaining flexible for doing the unpredictable and the unexpected.

By designing our days under God, one can avoid exercises in futility. Release yourself to make time for achieving salient goals.

 What can loom more satisfying than rich and fruitful productivity?

***Rekindled? Yes!***

# Day 2
## A FRESH LOOK AT PRIORITIES

### *Rx info-med*

On sabbatical in a seminary campus in England, Kathleen and I received an invitation to attend the school's commencement at which the Archbishop of Canterbury would address graduates and give out diplomas. We were to stay for lunch and the dedication of a recently constructed campus facility.

The new building was a student commons designed primarily for recreation. The Archbishop stated that a place to play (billiards, for example) carries importance second only to the chapel of a theological college. "I wish I had followed that priority program better," said the middle-aged prelate. He fervently hoped the divinity students and graduates would establish recreation as part of their lifestyle.

But the Archbishop himself had learned how to forget his work with its problems in order to stay emotionally healthy. He slopped pigs. Once home and away from the office, he donned high-top boots, skull cap, and weatherproof topcoat, and went to the pig sty to care for his animals.

This picture amuses me. Archbishop Robert Runcie's wife was a concert pianist, no doubt sophisticated in her tastes, perhaps fussy about keeping the house clean and tidy. Yet her clergyman husband returned night after night to the house from slopping pigs, complete with the characteristic odor of swine. One wonders how his spouse put up with the smelly clothes. Surely she required him to hang them in a place far distant from the kitchen and living room!

Mirth aside, the chief priest of English Anglicanism had the good sense to set aside time to renew himself from the pressures of a busy and often convoluted life.

Here's the problem: In our Western culture, where conditioning dictates guilt if we do not fill every minute with *worthwhile work* we often turn our backs on the necessity of *forgetting it all*.

Harry Hopkins, President Roosevelt's confidential advisor in World War II, modeled an answer to misplaced guilt feelings. A sick and dying man, Mr. Hopkins could work but a few hours daily, requiring him to identify only the most crucial concerns. The upshot? Hopkins "accomplished more than anyone else in wartime Washington" (Drucker 41).

God calls us to free our minds of the myth of indispensability. Ed Dayton believed we fear something will "slip through the cracks." He found a solution. "I tell myself, 'What happens when I'm off camping in the woods for three weeks? The world somehow gets along without me.... So you miss one out of ten important articles. So what?'" ("Time for All Things..." 21) Then maybe, after all, I can factor into my schedule time to re-create myself.

### *Rekindled? Yes!*

# Day 3

# A STRATAGEM FOR MANAGING TIME

### *Rx info-med*

A pastor friend lived in a parsonage attached to his Chicago church. Each morning he exited his home to enter the sanctuary and kneel at the altar. During his thirty minutes apart from people and noise, radio and TV, his notepad filled with assignments from the Inner Voice.

This daily pattern brought to my friend a whole new perspective on time management. The Sovereign Lord picked up the pieces of information heard from secretary and parishioners, from house calls and phone conversations, from the reading of the Word and devotional materials, and brought them to the pastor, wrapped in the cloak called *assignments*.

With divine control, time becomes the instrument of service and productivity and does not go to waste like water down the kitchen sink.

God has ways of telling us what to do and also what *not* to do. Elimination, part of the art of time management, releases us from push, rush and often time binds. Robert Louis Stevenson observed that he would be a genius if he knew what to omit. None of us needs be like writers who say too much.

What astonishes us about the psalmist's admonition to "be still and know that I am God" (Ps. 46:10) is the statement's context–war! (v. 9). Evidently the writer had so oriented himself to the voice of God that he could quiet himself to listen in the thick of battle. God's Spirit, the enabling Spirit, protects us from unnecessary busyness and clothes us in the garment of peace. Note these examples:

> A professional counselor closes his office door at noon to memorize Scripture verses from prepared cards. In Scripture he finds direction and energy to do his afternoon assignments.

> A woman walks to a nearby garden with a flowing fountain, just to sit quietly, listen to the sound of water, and become freshly aware of God's presence. Peace sends her on her way.

> Stanley Jones awakened each night to listen to the Inner Voice. At an Ashram, I heard Jones say that God gave him a reason to smile one night. Upon awakening, Dr. Jones said, "What do you want to say tonight, Lord?" "Nothing," came the answer. "Turn over and go back to sleep."

Silence is the sealed recording studio where we hear God. He speaks after the closed door drowns out all noise. Then the assignments come to bless and often surprise us. God Himself provides strength and ingenuity to use time to great benefit.

John Greenleaf Whittier writes about "the silence of eternity" in verse three of his hymn, "Dear Lord and Father of Mankind." Verses five and six spell out "the silence" and reveal victory over hassle and time fighting:

Drop Thy still dews of quietness
Till all our strivings cease:
Take from our souls the strain and stress,
And let our ordered lives confess
The beauty of Thy peace.

Breathe through the hearts of our desire
Thy coolness and Thy balm;
Let sense be dumb–let flesh retire;
Speak through the earthquake, wind, and fire,
O still small voice of calm!

The art of time management is the art of silence. No contemporary challenge looms more urgently than the ordering of our lives to make room for stillness. Not an easy challenge for, as someone observed, our culture has almost outlawed silence. Yet we must develop space for ridding ourselves of the onrush that so often defines the context of daily life and work. In quiet we lop off distractions, allowing the ear to expand to full listening range.

Thirty quiet minutes a day over the years will result in a resource complete with a divinely designed data bank and retrieval system.

***Rekindled? Yes!***

# Day 4
# HURRY IS THE DEVIL

### *Rx info-med*

"Hurry is not of the devil," goes the proverbial comment; "hurry is the devil."

Ponder the implications of rushing through a task only to live with emotional fatigue and embarrassing mistakes. Some personalities move along with remarkable haste as well as efficiency; however, most of us would do well to switch gears to a slower pace and thus become more accurate and often more creative. Imaginative answers require seeing all the way around a matter and that takes time.

Trying to beat the clock means push, push, push, and we break concentration because we think more about hurrying than focusing on the task at hand. Merely doing a task to get it done spells disaster, not only in terms of integrity in work but also in robbing one's mind of the delights of blessed labor. Can anyone imagine a Michelangelo speeding through a piece of sculpture? Look at his famous statue of David in Florence, Italy. Highest level art!

Meaning in the soul comes from doing a task well. And not just tasks such as building a house, even cleaning the house. How about connectional tasks such as relating to people? Fulfillment in the interpersonal context results from helping people work together, make decisions, and bring resolution to their problems—a species of sculpturing, unseen to be sure, but akin to creating a work of art. This kind of happy result to the soul is the consequence of associating openly, humbly, and therefore unhurriedly with people. Hurrying persons to decisions before they are ready creates rebellion and withdrawal. God designed time as the instrument of healthy interpersonal relationships.

We must resist hurry to remain healthy and whole. Yet many institutions and businesses engineer an architecture and environment that create a hurried atmosphere. Drive-through service, streams of bright colors to suggest fast movement, quick layout of food and drink—all spell scurry, what the Scots call *whirry*. Fast food is a paradigm of our age.

Observe these calculated dynamics to stay alive to the subtle manipulations of our restless world and thus to understand and react against temptation. And how do we react against the temptation to hurry?

Some prepare a sack lunch to eat in the park. Green grass and stately trees do not make one feel driven.

A seminary professor puts a cot in his office, closes the blinds at noon, and takes a nap.

An aircraft manufacturing executive defuses the mad rush by dictating memos for the next day on his way home from the office. No wonder he meets wife and kids at the close of the day with a clear mind and serene spirit.

When reading poetry, Wendell Berry, the Kentucky farmer and famous writer, says we should read slowly, thoughtfully.

Meanings, even feelings, dawn as the mind processes the words. Sometimes poetic messages even leap off the page.

### *Rekindled? Yes!*

# Day 5

## TIME AND INCENTIVE

### Rx info-med

Time without something interesting going on, without incentives, ushers boredom into our lives. With motivation, hours fill with substantive activity that enriches our sense of achievement.

*Psychology Today* polled 23,000 people to discover what they wanted in a job. Six priorities surfaced out of eighteen items rated: (1) enhance self-esteem, (2) accomplish something worthwhile, (3) learn something new, (4) develop skills and abilities, (5) have freedom on the job, (6) do what one does best. Of the eighteen items rated, job security came in eleventh place, money twelfth, and fringe benefits sixteenth.

Time in America, especially and in the Western world generally, is a valuable commodity when it is the carrier of meaning and not merely the instrument for making money. If time fills with inflexible routine, robbing laborers of personal initiative, meaninglessness sets in. Boredom means work no longer delights the worker.

Some companies have gone to flextime, a way employees can put in their eight hours somewhere between seven in the morning and six in the evening. A few organizations permit, even encourage, four ten-hour days. Enhancing freedom can help facilitate the six priorities above.

My son, James, a Hospice chaplain, worked with his fellow chaplains to establish a four-day week. Freeing up an entire day benefits the busy professionals in several ways. For example, it allows them uninterrupted computer time to write notes required by law on visits to patients in rest homes, stress release from road trips and focused listening to patients and colleagues, and in general a slower pace during the work week.

Flextime, one way to open workers to greater freedom and incentive, can introduce renewed enthusiasm, build up the work level in terms of productivity, and institute personal satisfaction. (For more on the six priorities above and flextime, see Potter.)

**Rekindled? Yes!**

# Day 6
# WHY DO I STAY SO BUSY?

### *Rx info-med*

Start with truth about yourself. If you project on the screen of your mind your mother's or father's idea of you, that image may attack you with the disease called perfectionism, pushing you to be an overachiever. Or if you live with an unsurrendered problem, you may try to cover the issue with doing too much, which results in workaholism. Your sensitivities and personality may drive you to try to fix everyone in need, one of the temptations of helping professionals. You may think of other reasons that account for living a too-busy life.

How well I remember the college president who told a professor who was in trouble with his marriage that he spent too much time at work. No wonder his wife felt cheated. Could he find time for her?

My father, serving as president of Seattle Pacific University, sat working behind his desk when I came into his office just to say hi. Suddenly, with no transition in conversation, he pointed his long bony finger across his desk and announced, "In this job I make decisions. Some turn out good, some so-so, and some fair-to-middlin'. I pray over each decision, get the best counsel available, then make my best determination." That made good sense to me, but he added something more: "Having made my decisions, I leave them. They're signed and sealed, as it were. That psychological stance leaves me free to lock my challenges in the office when I go home at night." I got the message: Dad did not take his problems home with him.

That put me in mind of professors and executives who take briefcases crammed with papers to their home desks, only to awake in the morning with a hangover headache.

To guarantee he did in fact lock his problems in the office, Dad developed a system of forgetting his administrative duties—hobbies. For years he collected patterned American glass, specializing in goblets. He bought books on the subject, mastered the stories of design and period of manufacture, even gave lectures on pressed glass. He got his mind completely off work. Sometimes he would take Mother to see fine china and crystal in the shops.

Later in life he collected stamps and coins. Again he educated himself, this time about collectible postage and money. Once when very busy at a week-long conference camp, he asked me to go to his desk where he housed bags of pennies. "Bring me a bag, any bag," he said. With his sharp eyes he examined pennies one by one. He knew the valuable ones by the tiny print indicating the mint where the pennies were made and the dates when they were manufactured. He learned, too, that to be truly engaged in hobbies, one must spend enough money to give them drawing power. Little investment, little engagement, he believed.

Can you find time and money for hobbies? They might slow you down and save your life.

### Rekindled? Yes!

# Day 7
# RHYTHMS

*Rx info-med*

A young lawyer, turned vice president of a seminary, said in his early days as an educational executive, "I'm learning the rhythms of this new job." Way to go because that's one of the keys both to job satisfaction and achievement.

To catch the ebb and flow, the give and take, the time for work and rest—that recipe goes a long way to make beautiful music of labor. Imagine music without rests, without time signatures! Gone the beat, the magic of harmonic progression, the delight of sound to the ear. Labor, to be rich and satisfying, becomes an art form.

The Psalms model rhythms for us. Note how often the word *rest*, or the term *wait* appears! Even *Selah*—perhaps meaning *stop, rest, take time to process*—emerges now and again. The pauses, evident in the soaring rhythms of Hebrew poetry, accentuate the cadence of the Old Testament hymn book. Some of the psalms worshipers sang as they marched in rhythm.

Years ago on a trip with my family, before the days of self-service, we stopped for gasoline at a service station in the mountains of California. A terribly busy young man rushed to my window. "Please fill the tank," I said.

He hurried to the pump, drove in the nozzle and proceeded to release the fuel into my tank, only to leave before
finishing with my car to go to the next car that drove up.
It became a kind of pattern of doing half tanks. Finally
one of the older employees said in a voice mixed with
steadiness and firmness, "Return to the first car; finish
that job before you go to a second." Disorder is helter-
skelter. No music there, only cacophony.

A tennis player got good guidance from her coach. He
noticed the anti-rhythmic character of her swings and
foot work. Her body language resulted in many a faulty
drive and serve. Pondering just how to guide his student,
he finally hit on an idea that worked. "I want you," he
said, "to swing to the rhythm of the Blue Danube Waltz."
Puzzled at first, she nonetheless played the melody in her
mind, then went onto the court to give it a try. Result?
She learned the flowing rhythms of good tennis playing.

You will experiment to discover the cadence of your own
soul. Once you take hold of the delay-and-activity, the
rise and fall, the give and take sequence that belongs to
you yourself, life and work will take on a lively art form
that pleases more than distresses, with the end-result of a
sense of completion and satisfaction.

**Rekindled? Yes!**

\*\*\*                \*\*\*                        \*\*\*

## WEEK'S SUMMARY POINT OF
## HOPE AND HEALING

To learn and implement your own rhythms for life and work is to make time your servant not your slave.

# WEEK 10

# REKINDLED: THE HEALING
# ROLE OF THE FAMILY

*A husband may beat his wife, but she will love him;*
*he may commit adultery, but she still loves him;*
*but if he ignores her with silence, she will leave him.*

—Anonymous

## Day 1
## FAMILY SUPPORT

*Rx info-med*

A revealing finding emerges from research on family support and survivors of serious disease. Those who enjoy strong family ties tend to have a much better chance of recovery from diseases such as cancer and cardiac maladies. Sufferers living with poor family support systems tend to feel themselves drawn away from life.

Loving affirmation in our families may literally be the difference between life and death. Psychosomatic studies demonstrate the clear relation between depression and physical illness. Love strangles and interrupts the common sequence—trauma followed by depression, then disease, and even death.

Support is not over-solicitous attention to one another. It is the ministry of presence. Like the ministry of Jim and Doris who have spent their lives *being there* with notes, letters, phone calls, money, anything we mean by personal attention. They traveled the earth, even in their eighties, to be with family and friends. Mere flattery would not work; these good people prove themselves authentic, sincere, servants.

They model support. Precisely how? They *listen.* Jim and Doris really don't talk much, but they always make time to lend an ear. *"Listening is silent love,"* the most eloquent kind of therapy and encouragement. Attentive hearing is a profound expression of selflessness and goes a country mile toward preventing burnout.

Jim and Doris *accept people just as they are.* When individuals come across full of self-pity, bitterness, and jealousy, never mind, accept them. Listening with full acceptance gives the joy that creates hope. Hope is medicine.

Jim and Doris also *refuse to pamper people.* When necessary they prod gently, subtly, patiently, but firmly. They never scold–that would serve only to deepen problems and add guilt feelings. Their aim is to bring family and friends to a point of clear thinking that opens windows to reality and a way out of trouble.

Jim and Doris, these examples of family and friend support, let you know they stand with you. Their lives spell empathy, affirmation, and support.

### *Rekindled? Yes!*

# Day 2

## FORGIVENESS

### *Rx info-med*

We can thank God for the current movement to expose abuse of wife, husband, child, or aged person. Our newspapers carry article after article about children sexually abused, verbally damaged, even beaten and battered. Such damage, the psychiatrists tell us, warps the emotional system and therefore creates confusion in the thought life. It plays havoc with self-identity and normal self-esteem. When the hurt goes inward, festering takes place, and depression can set in. Depression is often frozen anger.

Forgiveness is God's provision for handling anger. Family members who forgive one another stay together. One minister who has made himself available to hurting people for over half a century observes that he has rarely seen family problems unrelated to anger and an unforgiving spirit.

A wife involved in an affair lives with an ugly and festering load of guilt. She fears her husband will refuse forgiveness if she reveals what he does not know.

A father who has abused his son hesitates to come right out and ask forgiveness, the best possible step toward cure. Self-conscious about facing up to his sin and talking to his son about it, he tries favors to cover his wrong-doing, but they will not bring the longed-for reconciliation.

So what do children do when healing relationships with parents do not take place? They suffer through the years into adulthood where, in retrospect, they now know a lot more about what the inflicted pain does to the psyche and the personality. Can God break through such an impossible dilemma? Yes, a thousand times, yes. "For my father and my mother have forsaken me, but the Lord will take me up" (Ps. 27:10, RSV). Eugene Peterson renders this verse as follows: "My father and mother walked out and left me, but God took me in" (MSG). Peterson shows the struggle of the soul in the lines preceding verse 10 where the hurting son or daughter pleads with God: "You've always been right there for me; don't turn your back on me now. Don't throw me out, don't abandon me; you've always kept the door open." Then the climax of the paragraph, "My father and mother walked out and left me, but God took me in." Clearly the psalmist had learned to find his therapy in God when his parents had not initiated reconciliation. And by implication the same holds true when children abuse parents.

How do we forgive those who hurt us? The Bible instructs us to love people who inflict pain (1 Pet. 3:9; Rom. 12:14; Matt. 5:44; Prov. 25:21). Giving cool water to enemies may not at first be very inspiring, but great reward comes when we experience forgiveness and thus see what it does to bring comfort and sustain a sense of well-being.

Write this down: Only God grants grace to take the first step toward forgiving and receiving forgiveness. Yes, we may get encouragement from fellow Christians to take that first step, and yes, we may get help from an empathetic counselor, pastor, or priest. But when God's Spirit Himself grants us grace, whatever the antecedents, peace invades our soul.

When that release comes, a whole new sense of understanding and compassion for offenders shapes our attitude. The Spirit of God loosens the tenacious grip of resentment and resolves conflict to bring *shalom*. That very *shalom* wields profound power for healing burnout.

### *Rekindled? Yes!*

# Day 3

# FAMILY LOVE

## Rx info-med

Real live affection releases family members to meaning-ful relatedness and genuine joy. Mere sentimental love will not do that. Practical, gut-level love we see stopped in pictures like these:

*A school boy, robbed of his mother's nurturing love, cannot focus on class assignments. His mom suffers from psychosomatic ailments but resists treatment, suffering fear of what the doctor may discover. She could get help but will not.

*Here is a husband who cannot live with freedom and joy in his home because of his cold and distant wife. He suffers a serious spin-off: He cannot perform his duties in the workplace with the kind of proficiency that would give him appropriate job pride. A troubled heart may well create preoccupation with the problem, preventing resourcefulness in the work setting.

*In another family, the husband cannot tolerate his el-derly in-laws who have come to live in his house. Why did his wife insist on caring for her parents this way? How can the family develop caring relation-ships?

An exciting movement in the health-delivery community is *holistic medicine.* In one clinic the doctor listens to the *whole* story. Family members participate to fill in the chinks, clear the air of tensions and misunderstandings, and paint a completed picture. Once the physician makes him/herself aware of this larger family portrait, he or she patiently opens channels to restore free-flowing love. The doctor knows harbored resentments can cause major disease; she or he knows also that love can put resentments into perspective. The physician knows still further that once the emotional hang-ups come to resolution, physical ailments have a better chance to heal. Experts tell us traditional medical practice of drug and surgical remedies may not meet the complete therapeutic needs of a patient. Often primary therapy must come from the family. The code name for that remedy is love.

Love therapy begins with guileless friendship. Often couples say of their loved spouse, "He's/she's my best friend." Such intimate friendship comes from the heart; it lifts one above language and logic. It reflects a deeply meaningful relationship.

When family members are taken for granted, something very fundamental threatens friendship. When, however, we relate to one another with respect and attention, self-images climb and freedom leading to authentic *befriending* kicks in. Interestingly, disease can reverse into health when a sense of acceptance pervades the subconscious mind and comes to outward expression.

The grandest happiness is knowledge that we are loved, loved for who we are, no matter what our faults or idiosyncrasies. Modern psychotherapy says the same thing when its authorities announce that love has power to cure many a disorder, including burnout.

## *Rekindled? Yes!*

# Day 4

# INDEPENDENCE

## *Rx info-med*

Two contrasting stories follow. The one reveals a generous-minded husband who declared, "I wish my wife would spend more money on the clothes she would like to get for herself." Enjoying enough money to buy without guilt feelings goes a long way toward giving a woman independence.

The contrasting story is about a woman who kept accounts for herself and her husband; she poured over the books with the fierceness of Dickens' Scrooge. Though the two lived in a gorgeous Florida retirement home, complete with indoor pool, her husband felt imprisoned. He could spend only so much money, and her attitude said, "Only on purchases I approve." No room there for meeting the needs of his own self-governing instincts!

The first narrative is a metaphor for the self-reliance a fortunate wife relished, not only in terms of resources, but also of the sheer enjoyment she experienced in the whole of her life, the workplace included. That good woman ran a bookstore and spread laughter and enthusiasm to every customer. Clearly she came from a home that believed in freedom. The second story describes a man irritable and complaining, frustrated and in irons.

Perhaps his fear of illness was a spin-off from his imprisoned spirit, a heart cry issuing from crushed personhood.

God created us autonomous. Insightful teachers encourage the self-legislative spirit in their students. How well I recall my Scottish professor of theology saying to us students, "Develop your independence!" He himself modeled that freedom-of-thought posture in lectures and published writing.

And how well I remember F. F. Bruce, one of my mentors, declaring in private consultation, "Come to your own conclusion, a conclusion you yourself believe." We had been discussing the much debated authorship of certain books of the New Testament.

St. Paul says that "where the Spirit of the Lord is, there is freedom" (II Cor. 3:17). Take careful notice of the proviso, "where the Spirit of the Lord is...." Suppose the wife in the above story overspends, thus robbing both herself and her husband of enough money to live on–such behavior does not reflect operating in the context of the Spirit. The bookkeeper who shackled her husband with limitations certainly has much to learn about the freedom of the Spirit. Come to think about it, prostituting our God-given freedom only results in loss of the independence we are made for.

If you have trouble finding that balance, notice verse 18 of the 2 Corinthians 3 passage where Paul seems to extend his hand of sympathy to those in process of learning about liberty in the Spirit. He says we "are being changed into his likeness from one degree of glory to another; for this comes from the Lord who is Spirit." Thank you, St. Paul, for letting us know we can be patient with ourselves as we learn from experience how liberty in the Spirit works.

Strive then for independence in the framework of the Spirit's guidance. That will go a long way toward preventing burnout.

### *Rekindled? Yes!*

# Day 5

# A SENSE OF PLACE

### *Rx info-med*

Fortunate is the man who comes home to a wife eager to see him. Happy the woman who knows her spouse loves her deeply and wants to be with her. One's home is one's castle, guarded round about by the moat of privacy and comfort.

Paul Tournier, that gifted Swiss psychotherapist of a past generation, took pains to make his clients feel at home. For example, he loved building a fire, placing two comfortable chairs at the fireplace–doing his best to make his patient feel at home. He knew this sense of being-at-home is in itself therapeutic. Natural healing takes place where comfort-in-depth enters the soul. The Christian home, a foretaste of heaven, supplies consolation.

To make home a retreat where one experiences refurbishing of mind and heart, makes possible facing the workaday world with its threats of burnout. An army officer, with a little family, moved from campsite to campsite, from one residence to another. "I'm sorry you don't have a home of your own," said a family friend to the little daughter. "Oh," she said, "we do have our own home. Every house we live in we make into a home."

That small girl is fortunate. She has a mother on whose shoulder she can cry when she comes home from school after a boy hits her or the teacher scolds her. Her mother listens and talks in comforting words and tone.

A wife who has time to hear her husband's trials and threats, and who makes it her habit to speak in faith-building words, brings solace and resolution to her mate. A woman who can unload a heart full of aches on her spouse, a companion who lifts with a word of inspiration and manly style, knows she lives in a protected place, the right place, her true home.

What makes a home a place of security? Edith and Francis Schaeffer traveled a good bit. She made it her practice to take a pretty table cloth, candle, china, and silver to make a home wherever they went. They might end up eating at a box as their table, but the cloth covered it, the candle burned in place, the table was set to re-create a sense of home.

Perhaps little things go a long way toward making a place of comfort and security. When my father broke both his legs, mother took pains to bring his food on a decorative tray with a single rose in a vase, along with beautifully presented food. Dad, a busy pastor, continued to administer the church from his bed, the phone close by. With the passage of time, he enjoyed enough healing to get to his feet with crutches, later with a cane. He learned to do weddings seated on a high stool. Mother's TLC was altogether behind my father's ability to keep going under the most challenging circumstances. Foundational security characterized his home, the launch pad for climbing a very difficult mountain victoriously.

### *Rekindled? Yes!*

# Day 6
## LIFE'S LABORATORY

*Rx info-med*

The family is a working laboratory for learning how life works. In the family unit we learn the secrets of effective living.

How do we go about this all-important enterprise?

**Live together in love.** Love and mutual respect allow each person to be himself or herself. Such a circle of kith and kin does not construct a utopia where only perfect people exist; good families allow one another to make mistakes and receive rewards for worthy accomplishment. Herein lies the warp and woof of life-learning skills. The confidence and conditioning generated in such an atmosphere is premium fuel providing energy to participate in life with efficiency, enthusiasm, and fulfillment.

**Live together in fun.** Wholesome families learn the liberation of variety and balance. We cannot work all the time; games have their place, too. So does teasing, which gently and lovingly exposes our inconsistencies. Over-seriousness, like artifice, results in warped perspective. A run along the beach, a swim in the pool, a story by the fireside–all and more provide that family relaxation, recreation and merriment without which we cannot live normal lives.

**Live together in a real world.** Family life teaches realistic expectations. To reach too high means failure and disappointment; to bend too low results in lack of challenge and boredom. Family dialog assists in discovering that middle ground, which is realism, and teaches us that life does not consist of people who smile beautifully all the time, smell like a flower garden, and make money effortlessly. Many a college graduate summarizes his or her consensus on this issue: "It's a lot harder out there than we were given to believe in university." Sound family living and talk project the nature of the real world.

Live together in readiness to help one another cope. Look at these typical scenarios:

> When a member of the family comes home absolutely exhausted, sensitive families empathize with the fatigue. It may have been caused by someone's mean spirit or rejection at the office.

> When one divorces himself or herself from active involvement, disappointment may have been the culprit giving rise to the isolation. Suggest time for understanding talk or permission to take a nap.

> When one turns critical, even sarcastic, enthusiasm may well have been dampened by a hurried and harried work day. Encourage unloading the frustration.

When a member of the family yields to temptation, the resulting bad behavior calls for kindly but firm dialog.

Take this last scenario for fuller thought. Look at teenage drinking, for example. Much parent burnout results from problems with their children. Often young people do not know what happens to the brain with alcohol intake. Normal brain development, especially the prefrontal cortex and hippocampus, suffers and can lead to chronic cognitive and behavioral problems, in addition to alcoholism in adult years. Suppose the family reads together the research findings on teen drinking in the article, "Alcohol and the Brain: Buzz Kill" (Paturel) and in the magazine's editorial, "The Adolescent Brain" (Brey). The forthright and easy-to-understand language makes this crucial data accessible and furnishes the material for thoughtful family discussion.

\*\*\*            \*\*\*            \*\*\*

The laboratory training a family provides prepares persons for happy living in a harsh world and sends young people off to school, work, and marriage with coping skills. No household prepares everyone completely against burnout threats, but an alert family supplies the timbers that go into building strong emotional and spiritual personalities.

### *Rekindled? Yes!*

# Day 7
## PRIVACY

***Rx info-med***

Today's conditioning to openness is both good and bad. Learning to share strain and stress is good; however, we can never force privacy to yield its needed secrets lest we rob people of their dignity. A native sense of reserve characterizes normal human beings. Secrets must come to discovery at their own speed.

See the whispered delights before Christmas, birthdays, and Valentine's Day as a metaphor of our need to keep secrets. Secrets enjoy a wholesome privacy that says we belong to ourselves and like to create our own surprises. In the larger sphere of confidentiality, who has not confided in a pastor or friend something not intended for everyone but may in fact be revealed at a later and more appropriate time.

Family members who pry create over-dependency; they can also inflict hurt, not only momentarily but in the long run by robbing one of a sense of their full identity. Employers who must know everything make servile employees. Drive vanishes when personhood suffers threat.

Burnout takes place when the rewards derived from personal initiative vanish. If what I do only serves someone else's ends, fulfillment evades me. I must have the freedom to do it my way; get the job done in my own imaginative way. My accomplishment is my reward.

When families and workplaces succeed in cultivating personhood, burnout suffers a major defeat. The positive feedback acts as fuel to generate health, energy, ideas, and achievements. Enthusiasm comes from the sense that *I* can do important tasks well. The private *I,* when kept intact and encouraged, becomes happily productive.

Every family should read Paul Tournier's *Secrets.* This little book reveals the need of children to have secrets that play a part in developing their distinct individuality. Maturity, Tournier says, lies partially in the freedom to keep and share secrets. He believes his own success as a counselor relates in important ways to his reserve with clients. He does not permit himself self-gratifying curiosity about their secrets.

God helping us, we will learn the balance of privacy and openness, and the skill of relating to both with dignity and respect. When we find ourselves in authority–parenting, supervising in the work place, chairing a committee–we have no right to invade the private world of others; we do have the obligation to invite both revelation and creativity with the spirit of Christ who seemed to know when and where to communicate the hidden mysteries of the Kingdom (Mark 4:34; John 7:10; cf. Gal. 2:2).

Lord, grant us grace to listen and to respect.

### *Rekindled? Yes!*

\*\*\*                \*\*\*                \*\*\*

## WEEK'S SUMMARY POINT OF
## HOPE AND HEALING

**Families and circles of friends that love in song, word, and prayer know heaven's joy.**

# WEEK 11

# REKINDLED: FACING FEAR

Don't fret and worry. Instead of worrying, pray. Let petitions and praises shape your worries into prayers, letting God know your concerns. Before you know it, a sense of God's wholeness, everything coming together for good, will come and settle you down. It's wonderful what happens when Christ displaces worry at the center of your life.

—Phil. 4:6-7, MSG

Let me assert my firm belief that the only thing we have to fear is fear itself.

—Franklin Delano Roosevelt
First inaugural address
4 March 1933

Chapters 11, 12 and 13 focus on the three dragons: guilt, anger, and fear. No counselor fails to observe the three as enemies of peace and joy. In fact, they may be chief causes of burnout. Guilt is the weight of the past, anger the burden of the present, and fear our worry about the future. We consider these in reverse order, fear in this week, anger in the next, and guilt in the final set of readings.

# Day 1

## PERSEVERATION

### *Rx info-med*

Perseveration, when activated in the brain-damaged, is uncontrollable rut thinking. Twenty-one year old Betty's brain suffered damage by a smallpox vaccination in infancy, the needle unsterilized. Betty received a valentine from a secret pal and cannot quit talking about it: "Look at my valentine. Who do you think sent it? Doesn't the handwriting look like Auntie Jane's?" Betty's mother called this repetitive behavior "perseveration." On Betty goes, repeating herself nonstop, until her caregiver intervenes.

A species of perseveration (pur-sev-er-a-shun) strikes the burnout victim. Insecurity puts a stranglehold on spontaneity, planning suffers paralysis, thought goes in circles. Phrases go round and round in one's head, the victim urgently hoping and trying to find a way out of the nonstop merry-go-round.

Fear that one cannot perform at work, school, or home has become the dynamic. This dread generates preoccupation with details, slows the normal sequence of activity, and interrupts goal achievement.

Confusion and paralysis stem from fear of others. What will the board think? How will the senior partner react?

Who of my coworkers will respond to me negatively? A normal amount of pre-imaging is, of course, natural and needed, not only for working with one's colleagues, but also for correcting mistakes and inept behaviors. But carried to extreme, pre-imaging becomes perseveration.

How can we stop the onslaught of repeated, worried, and fearful thoughts? We begin to find the answer in active caring. Face your enemies, real (and supposed). Do them good professionally and personally. Express your benevolent spirit covertly in words, overtly in cooperative support.

### *Rekindled? Yes!*

# Day 2

## FEAR OF FAILURE

### *Rx info-med*

On one occasion Steve Allen's TV interview guest, a doctor, said, "The only two really instinctive fears in people are the fear of loud noises and the fear of falling." Then the physician asked Steve, "What are you afraid of?"

Comedian Steve Allen replied, "I have a great fear of making a loud noise while falling."

Most of us have conquered the two infancy fears, but anxieties about failure rear their ugly heads in low moments. We rehearse past mistakes and relive embarrassing moments. Usually we can laugh, but in burnout capacities get locked up in the prison of ourselves. The desk piled with work paralyzes rather than stimulates us to action.

How do we get this way? We suffer displeasure with ourselves. The point of unhappiness does not always surface readily, and self-preoccupation takes over the search. In this mood we run the risk of inflicting problems on ourselves as well as others; the resultant fears may render us ineffective.

We need not, however, allow fears to unnerve us. When tempted into the abyss of self-absorption, we can (1) recognize the tendency as a sign of threat calling us to attack it. We can find help by (2) vigorous exercise such as tennis, racquetball, swimming, walking. Caught during the initial stages, fatigue and fear toxins yield to the body's own tranquilizing action in a good workout. In this relaxed position we can (3) listen to ourselves and expect nature and God to show us the true problem. When the clouds separate to reveal the issue (4) the mind contents itself with clear thought, meaningful conversation, food, drink and sleep. Overeating and oversleeping, sometimes under-eating and insomnia, indicate abnormal emotional involvement.

Recognition, exercise, listening, and healthy habits go a long way toward coping with the threat of failure and burnout.

***Rekindled? Yes!***

# Day 3

## OVERCOMING WORRY

### *Rx info-med*

Worry is a kind of fear. The word *worry* comes from the Anglo-Saxon for *choke* or *strangle*. What a clear picture of the very thing that robs us of life, Life with a big L!

Job 3:25 tells us how worry can do its evil work: "For the thing that I fear comes upon me, and what I dread befalls me." Eugene Peterson puts this insightful verse into perspective:

> Instead of bread I get groans for my supper, then leave the table and vomit my anguish. The worst of my fears has come true, what I've dreaded most has happened. My repose is shattered, my peace destroyed. No rest for me, ever—death has invaded my life.

Horrific images can grip us and we feel like they will never end. Worriers get into trouble because trouble gets into them. And some of them—we call these people *worry warts*—attract trouble like a magnet draws filings.

In fact, fear can actually make one choke, like the woman who couldn't swallow. Her pastor worked with her until she saw the psychosomatic dynamics of her worry. Success followed her new awareness. Choking on food and drink stopped, and normal swallowing returned.

Worry can quickly inject burned-out feelings in the mind, choking out vibrancy, the excitement that motivates us to get things done. One cure is to think thoughts antagonistic to worry. Psychologists sometimes counsel handling depression by challenging dark thoughts with opposing pictures. Yes. Choose, for example, a Thomas Kinkade painting with his famous light motif, or recall a trip to the ocean, or a vacation in the mountains.

We do not have to be rocked back and forth on the sea of worry. We can, rather, generate thoughts that create feelings of peace and calm. Conditioning ourselves with such picture material, as part of our daily lifestyle, has great benefits, especially because we know we will face the inevitable upcoming storms of life.

Best of all, the God who is love stands with us in the throes of adverse experience. St. John tells us perfect love casts out fear because fear signals punishment but love favors us with God's comfort, strength, and mercy. Isaiah 35:3-4 promises help:

> Strengthen the weak hands, and make firm the feeble knees. Say to those who are of a fearful heart, "Be strong, fear not! Behold, your God will come with vengeance, with the recompense of God. He will come and save you." (RSV)

Yes, we must cooperate with God's healing Presence, which we can do in several ways. First, consciously see yourself conqueror until the subconscious mind kicks in with spontaneous positive reaction to daily threats. Second refuse negative, debilitating thoughts. Remember that, according to some research, barely 2 or 3 percent of our anxieties materialize. Research also shows that those

who watch a lot of TV may enhance fear-oriented per-
ceptions. Third, recall too that God fights for and with us
against evil forces, a theological fact documented by the
cross and resurrection. The New Testament says the resurrected Christ lives in us by His Spirit to maintain victorious abundant Life. In this regard the Lutheran doctrine
of the Presence of Jesus in the Lord's Supper—He is *in,
with, under,* and *around* the bread and wine—is analo-
gous to the Spirit's Presence *in, with, under,* and *around*
you and me.

## Rekindled? Yes!

# Day 4

## ENEMIES AS OPPORTUNITIES

### *Rx info-med*

Enemies can unnerve us. We stand in awe, even down-right fear, of them on occasion. Some enemies are people, some are circumstances, others are conditions.

Our primary challenge relates to attitude. Seeing enemies as opportunities is the secret. Not an easy assignment! View opposition as a prod to growth and advancement in problem-solving skills. Enemies bring into bold relief creative possibilities, possibilities we might otherwise miss.

Who can resist the story of the mathematics professor who put two historically unsolved problems on a final examination? One of the bright fellows in the class saw the problems, called them a challenge rather than an enemy, asked the professor for time beyond the two-hour limit, and would you believe actually solved one of the two sticklers! A classic mathematical dilemma yielded to the bright mind of an eager possibility-thinking student.

Stories like this abound and we all love them because who doesn't like the adventure of standing up to an un-solvable enigma and solving it! This kind of possibility thinking positions us to assume command of aggravating situations. Anxiety sets in when "the enemy" takes command; exhilarating mood takes hold when adventurous challenge becomes the General.

With clear and sturdy thinking, God's Word enables us to live above, not under, our circumstances.

Nail this principle down with three ways to see problems and problem people:

*See enemies as instruments of your development.* View them as friends. E. Stanley Jones, that remarkably productive world evangelist, believed his critics were the unpaid guardians of his soul. He listened to them, considered carefully their critiques of his ministry, and implemented legitimate suggestions. He grew under criticism. Challenges prevent stunted growth.

*See yourself capable of creative coping.* The doctrine of enabling in the Scriptures assures us of the equipping Presence that brings victory. God makes us bigger than our antagonists. His Kingdom within us opens our eyes to options, gives us the capacity to focus on best choices, and provides energy to implement a determined plan of action. Each of us has far greater potential than we realize.

*See your wider opportunities.* Intentional prayer, creative listening, and innovative design suggest an infinite number of approaches to grasping winning strategies. Let me share a single example from my own work: A telephone call to a wise man put me at ease in a preaching situation where I suspected opposition. I discovered the mind-set of the people whom I had been called to serve. My thoughts moved out of neutral into first gear, then proceeded rapidly into second and third, resulting in a wonderfully productive week.

A carefully planned meeting can yield interest; a well-written letter itemizing precise needs can bring answers; thoughtfully selected personnel can brainstorm to profit. And part of the fun of living in this electronic age lies in the enormous range of communication possibilities for opening creative doors leading to exciting planning and accomplishment.

In summary, see enemies as opportunities for looking at options, designing for growth, and achieving for great good.

***Rekindled? Yes!***

# Day 5

# ATTACKING FEAR WITH LOVE

## *Rx info-med*

The famous psychotherapist Karl Menninger discovered his clinic produced minimal results. He called his staff together to ask them to add love to their daily rounds. Little deeds of kindness, projections of care and warmth could show evidence of authentic concern, genuine and appropriate affection. The result? Hospital workers no longer saw patients as things or numbers. Therapy charts showed major improvements in person after person. Karl Menninger, sensitive guide that he was, hit a home run.

No wonder Dr. Menninger declared, "Love is the medicine for the sickness of the world." Behind this powerful comment lies an equally powerful psychiatric discovery: The root of most hang-ups centers in the inability to receive or give love. Teach people to love, and meaningful and liberated living follows (Jones, *Word Became Flesh* 88-89).

Can love really handle ordinary everyday fears? Yes. I cannot live for long in fear of those who genuinely love me, nor will persons fear me for very long if I truly love them. Even animals respond positively to love, negatively to fear. And when I love even myself, fears about myself vanish to bring freedom.

Take this example: A prayer list of needy persons will soon evolve into a love list. Deliberately put on your list authority figures who threaten you; then watch your paraanoia leave and simon-pure regard emerge. Sincere praying for someone issues in love for that person.

Activating this principle inevitably helps us sense that even the abrasive people we do not like to be around are crying for help, for as the old proverb goes, "Any cry is a cry for help." Fear of the too-bold multiplies fear in us and often in the people who threaten us. Scientists tell us animals respond emotionally. Fear elicits in them attack responses, biting, for example. It sheds light on why dogs like to nuzzle rather than bite someone who projects warmth. Fear responses intensify another's fears; conversely, love signals put us at ease.

The Scriptures communicate quite openly the genius of love as the instrument of joyful living as over against fearful living. For instance, note the imperative call in Ephesians 5:18: "… be filled with the Spirit." God's Spirit is love. First John 4:7-21 shows the power of love to overcome fear and maintain happy relationships. Peterson, typical of his interpretive gifts, grasps this grand truth, seen in three sample verses from the John 4 passage:

> My beloved friends, let us continue to love each other since love comes from God. Everyone who loves is born of God and experiences a relationship with God. (vv. 7-8)

> My dear, dear friends, if God loved us like this, we certainly ought to love each other. No one has seen God, ever. But if we love one another, God dwells deeply within us, and his love becomes complete in us—perfect love! (vv. 11-12)

If anyone boasts, "I love God," and goes right on hating his brother or sister, thinking nothing of it, he is a liar. If he won't love the person he can see, how can he love the God he can't see? The command we have from Christ is blunt: Loving God includes loving people. You've got to love both. (vv. 20-21)

## *Rekindled? Yes!*

# Day 6

## COURAGE

### *Rx info-med*

"Screw your courage to a sticking place," cried Lady Macbeth in answer to her husband's fearful question, "...if we fail?" Her complete answer exposes her bravery: "Screw your courage to the sticking place and we'll not fail" (*Macbeth* act I, sc. 7, l.54).

How do we "screw our courage to the sticking place" in the face of odds bigger than ourselves? Conditioning during calm times surely helps prepare us for the rough experiences ahead.

Just what are those conditioning components? Note four over-lapping constituents:

*Tenacity* develops as we learn to finish tasks. We must, yes *must*, teach our children stick-to-itiveness. Homework begun calls for homework completed. And for busy adults, called from many directions, bombarded with stimuli, we must nonetheless bring to terminus what we commence. The resultant full-circle feeling not only rewards us with a job well done, it also builds muscle and courage, to make it the habit of our lives.

*Mettle*, the ingrained capacity to meet strain and stress, increases by watching examples of valor as well as by facing up to difficult situations. Heroic models breed mettle in others. We can model stoutheartedness, thus inspiring those around us. A bold spirit grows by facing up to, not dodging, life's challenges that come with astonishing regularity, most especially in the workplace and at home.

*Resolution*, related and overlapping with tenacity and mettle, is the stubborn willingness to achieve goals. This skill materializes with a never-say-die attitude. The harder the challenge, the greater the girth added to existing muscle. God calls us to face contests resolutely with His promised help. Old Testament stories (David, for example) spell out the power of resolve.

*Spirit* fortifies one to continue against opponents, road blocks, and temptations and emanates from the Spirit of God. His Spirit furnishes us with determination when fear accosts us. The Hudson Taylor missionary stories can never cease to inspire us with spirit. Called to China's totally unpaved roads, paganism rampant, the name of Christ never articulated, Taylor and family, later with colleagues, carved their way though the torrents of impossibility and won! Fear? Many a time! Victory? Yes, by God's Spirit.

**Rekindled? Yes!**

# Day 7
## USES OF FEAR

***Rx info-med***

Fear has good sides. Look at just five.

*Fear protects us.* When threats loom, security comes under siege. Fear has the power to prod us to healthy self-defense. Onrushing traffic makes us stop to look both ways.

*Fear flies the caution flag.* At least one researcher found that people who watch a lot of TV introduce fright into their psyches. Television writers know that interest rises with shocking material. Not only do we need to help our children watch good movies and family-oriented programs, we do well to sift and sort for ourselves. In addition, in conversation at work or home, positive, happy topics sustain and build good conditioning.

*Fear serves a good purpose when it prods us to cry out against evil power structures.* When child porn scars innocent minds, we ought to be afraid for our children and we must move to constructive action. Interestingly, forthright opposition to evil, flowing from sure-of-your-ground motivation, does not in itself cause burnout. On the other hand, withdrawal from confrontation with evil gives rise to guilt and inner conflict which leads to fear and burnout.

*When fear threatens courage, it prompts us to stand tall.* An Arctic explorer, Frederick Johnson, spoke in unvarnished language when he observed that, "Worry does not empty tomorrow of its troubles—it empties today of its strength." Just think about that comment coming from an adventurer who knew about the threat of ice-floes, the gripping discomfort of frostbite, the unending white space with its power to blind, and the unforgivable cold that chills to the bone. John Milton wrote a priceless half-dozen words when he penned "… courage never to submit or yield" (*Paradise Lost* bk. 1, 1 105). Joshua, that adventure-driven Old Testament leader, possessed that kind of courage. He knew how to face the fear that yields to temptation to opt out: "I hereby command you: Be strong and courageous; do not be frightened or dismayed, for the Lord your God is with you wherever you go" (Josh. 1:9, NRSV). Consult your concordance for other references to strength and courage.

*Note the benefit of what the Bible calls "the fear of the Lord."* This Old Testament motif is the context for both personal valor and respect for God's moral law. Recall accounts such as David and Goliath—"the battle is the Lord's"—in which regard for the Almighty comes into clear and vivid view. Christians respond to His assignments as a soldier says yes to his or her commander. Highest consideration for God's power and law marks stalwart Christians. Saying no to the adrenalin-challenging opportunities and enemies of life means compromising values and often spoiling one's influence. More, to back off from God's sovereign Presence prognosticates unhealthy fear of God. But respect and reverence for the Creator is the foundation of an altogether healthy attitude toward the God of law and righteousness. That posture can only issue in reward and "the joy of the Lord, [which] is your strength" (Neh. 8:10).

*Rekindled? Yes!*

      ***          ***          ***

## WEEK'S SUMMARY POINT OF
## HOPE AND HEALING

**"...perfect love casts out fear..."**
**( 1 John 4:18, NRSV).**

# WEEK 12

# REKINDLED: CONVERTING ANGER

Man who gets angry quickly, gets old quickly.

—South Sea Islands proverb

My father … used to say, "I need my anger. It obliges me to
take action."
I think my father was pretty right. Anger arises, naturally,
to signal disturbing situations that might require action.
But actions initiated in anger perpetuate suffering.
The most effective actions are those conceived in the
wisdom of clarity.

—Sylvia Boorstein

## Day 1

## ANGER CONVERTED

*Rx info-med*

God designed basic human anger to create good. Rage
stimulates the brain, calling for alterations in body chemistry to propel us into remedial action.

A California mother lost her beautiful daughter when a
drunk driver used his vehicle as a battering ram. Today

that irate mother works effectively with authorities to stop one of the great social evils of our time.

That mother acts wisely because her redemptive activity serves to bring indignation to resolution. Unresolved anger can build and freeze into depression. It is a major factor in causing burnout.

Unthawed anger can cause illness, even contribute to death. Joe bitterly resented his arduous drive to and from daily employment; on a day off at the golf course, he dropped dead. No doubt death came as the result of a complex of factors, but anger seems to have been one of them.

How do we resolve and convert our anger into something constructive?

*Learn to recognize unremitting fury for what it is.* Become aware of how anger expresses itself. Freud believed depression was anger turned in on itself, what we might call iced-over rage. Little depressive thoughts and moods may arise from feelings that hide in the subconscious. To become aware of anger's expression is the knowledge that precedes therapeutic action.

*Translate your feelings of injustice into constructive activity.* People in the helping professions object inwardly and angrily to unfair action. They'd better! But they dare not leave interior anger boiling. The generated steam needs channeling, like writing an article to clear a misconception, raising tuition money for the young woman from deprived circumstances, or chairing the local chari-ty committee to correct misallocation of funds.

The Bible admonishes us not to let the sun go down on our wrath. We live fully, said Elizabeth Kubler-Ross, the famous Swiss-American physician, only after getting rid of anger.

### *Rekindled? Yes!*

# Day 2

## CURES OF HURT AND ANGER

### *Rx info-med*

We know that hurt and anger are close neighbors. Wounds can give birth to anger. Hurt and anger need to be exchanged for peace and love.

How do we exchange the bad feelings for the good?

*Recognize the benefits of hurt.* Sorrow may be as difficult to break through as the Great Wall of China, but it can become a door opening on revelation. When grief knocks, expect fresh discoveries. When we look in the direction of the knock an opening comes into view.

Anger at life's disappointments can blind us to the door in the wall. Conversely, readiness to see exposes the doorway through which looms a horizon of opportunity and often unspeakable beauty and splendor. Walk through the door into the hope of starting over again.

*Know God stands ready to give you comfort.* Jesus announced this truth in a beatitude: "Blessed are those who mourn, for they shall be comforted" (Matt. 5:4, RSV). Eugene Peterson brings fresh perspective to this ancient proverb with his paraphrase: "You're blessed when you feel you've lost what is most dear to you. Only then can you be embraced by the One most dear to you" (Matt. 5:3 MSG). Jesus knew that God eagerly and readily provides solace when sorrow strikes, with its destabilizing effect, at the heart of life. Willing souls open their arms to the Presence of Christ, who graces us with consolation.

*The Word of God is medicine.* Wounds call for treatment. The Bible, known to receptive souls for its healing powers, dispenses therapy to hurting persons. Written to people in pain, the Scriptures breathe the very medicinal power of God.

The Bible is filled with literally thousands of promises of His mercy and comfort. Notice just three examples from the Psalms in the *Message*:

> God makes everything come out right, he puts victims back on their feet. (Ps. 103:6)

> Oh, thank God—he's so good! His love never runs out. All of you set free by God, tell the world! Tell how he freed you from oppression, then rounded you up from all over the place, from the four winds, from the seven seas. (Ps. 107:1-3)

> God holds me head and shoulders above all who try to pull me down. I'm headed for his place to offer anthems that will raise the roof! Already I'm singing God-songs; I'm making music to God. (Ps. 27:6)

When hurt and angry, go to a quiet place where you can engage yourself in meditation. Read the Book with an open heart. Ponder the fresh insights that come from the Medicine of Truth. Then watch clouds lift and observe your return to normalcy.

### *Rekindled? Yes!*

# Day 3

## HEALERS GET HEALED

### *Rx info-med*

Deeply hurt people often find themselves working through anger very slowly. Acts of love assist and hasten the process. A loving lifestyle gives daily therapy to persons in pain, averting anger buildup.

The selfless turning away from our own injustices to concentrate on others has great power to heal. *Healers get healed.*

A pastor who studies the art of kindness fills his days ministering to bring damaged people relief. He does favors for the unloved and lonely, sends a short note to someone in grief, calls on another requiring counsel to put into motion comforting and strengthening influences. No wonder he sleeps soundly at night!

The genius of kindness is self-giving. A patient with mental illness rejected her young chaplain's offer of candy because she sensed the chocolates served as a substitute for giving himself. Jesus gave no money, food or clothes. He detected deeper hungers for love and longing for companionship. Jesus met these elemental needs for friendship not by activism but by the simple ministry of presence. He showed interest in people, which made them feel worthwhile. Gentleness, a caring spirit, concern, and empathy all speak eloquently from our Lord's life.

A therapist commenting on teenage suicide states that anger at God gets at the root cause of self-destruction. "Why have you made me this way? Why have you put me in this environment? Why have you created me at all?" Suicide is the ultimate revenge against the Creator.

We can bring moderating influences to bear on despondent lives, sometimes making a heaven out of a hell. This service won't make a headline, but it can translate someone's restlessness into calm and blackness into sunshine. In the process our own anger, self-pity, and egocentricity come to release.

**Rekindled? Yes!**

# Day 4

# ANGER AND A NEW JOB

### *Rx info-med*

One study shows Americans changing jobs ten times in the course of a lifetime. Anger can lift its ugly head in the context of major changes. Change may breed insecurity; in contrast, job stability fosters security, sometimes too easily. Maladjustments drain energies; if constructive, positive thoughts do not keep pace with emotional investment, burnout may ensue.

Sometimes an administrator or overseer sees you more advantageously placed in a new role. The alteration may cause torment, even paranoia (e.g., Why is my boss putting me in *that* job?). Working through the new and perhaps foreign territory, getting on with the fresh responsibilities—these tasks and more—can make one feel maladjusted. Moreover, a new assignment often carries hurt. Who likes to leave happy coworkers and familiar procedures? Breaking bonds does not seem to hold much promise.

A fresh opportunity may seem exciting, but if it requires moving to another place, it can also be daunting. The mobility rate charts in the United States show high turnovers; some communities clock-up very high percentages. Children suffer as they leave friends and school. Couples chafe under the necessity of settling into different homes and into communities with new neighbors and a diverse shopping environment. Family finances groan under the burden of buying and selling real estate. Adjustments to the local cost-of-living index can prove more challenging than expected. A new environment requires the development of fresh coping skills.

Short-fused people find adjustment hard, yet Christian disciplines and God's grace provide the working resources of help. The Spirit promises the fruit of the Spirit—love, joy, peace, patience, kindness, goodness, faithfulness, gentleness, and self-control. These disciplines may take time and effort to materialize.

Then there's the exercise of faith which means tapping expedient resources. *Remembering*, for example, is a storehouse of supply. An altogether important word in the Bible, the term *remember* calls to mind God's sure and effective help in the past. He has never forsaken His people; He will meet our needs now. Upon still further reflection, we see something of the blueprint God has for our lives. This picture-in-the-making prompts us to see the present as a step further down the road to fulfilling God's plan for our lives. God the Father guides and provides for His children.

Change may well be a mind-stretching, faith-challenging experience—just what builds character and prods to creative living and puts fresh energy into us. The *Paraclete*, the One alongside us, the Spirit Himself will provide capacity to adjust with grace and find His intended fulfillment.

### Rekindled? Yes!

# Day 5

## TACKLING LEADER ISOLATION

### *Rx info-med*

Leaders suffer isolation, to more or less degree, for many reasons. They may think beyond others, speeding ahead on the fast track, thus separating themselves from those who feel like tag-along people. Leaders dream great dreams, making some who are preoccupied with routine duties feel insignificant. But the front man or woman who serves well listens carefully, yet often overseers feel so threatened they cannot hear the real heart cries of their employees. After all, directors who get along with their personnel know they must accept people just as they are, not as they wish them to be. The supervisory position calls for empathy, which may seem for all the world to come in short supply. Few followers accept fully and identify completely with authority figures.

With the loneliness that goes along with headship comes dissociation in the social circle. Hurt and rage may enter the leader's soul. *Why am I treated this way? After all, I support my workers; I help provide their salaries; I discipline myself to act upbeat whether I feel like it or not. Why do they avoid me?*

Some chiefs drown the sense of exile with alcohol or drugs, but in so doing double their sense of imprisonment. Others try to find their need for nurturing in an affair but end up in disgrace. Some take on a kind of desperate talkativeness, only to find ostracism increased.

No escape mechanism works. In fact, negative techniques end in double failure: isolation worsens, anger accumulates. So how does the chief cope?

**Accept the cleavage as a cross to bear.** Jesus did. People born in sin did not like to hear the truth from His lips. Nonetheless, He revealed the difference between right and wrong. By the same token, a CEO may well feel the sting of isolation when leading his or her organization along the best, though very different, path.

**Accept the result of cross bearing—resurrection hope.** My friend Dave McKenna served as President of Seattle Pacific College. He envisioned turning that great institution into a greater place of learning by making it a university. I can still hear one of the faculty members speaking in a skeptical tone: "This place is no university; universities have schools, not mere departments." This view, no doubt shared by many, did not bring a halt to Dr. McKenna's dream. Seattle Pacific University came into being, schools developed, and enrollment expanded into the thousands. The cross of hard work turned into a grand resurrection.

**Wisdom dictates that leaders push others up the ladder ahead of them.** Humble leaders get along with their people. Wise pastors invite guest ministers who can preach better than they do. More, ministers who hand responsibilities over to potential leaders enter the arena of the much-needed leadership development enterprise. Inspire others to envision bigger, enlarge their store of knowledge, and develop fresh and creative ways of getting things done.

**Remind yourself of the loving response of your people.** True, despite your best efforts at empathy, something of a wall exists between you and your people due in part, of course, to respect, which every leader needs. Yet
the honor that comes with it finds expression in plaques and portraits, commendation at banquets, even a warm handshake in the hallway. And the material gifts (a gourmet dinner, a remembrance from an overseas trip, a new book) often seem to come gratis nonstop. When superiors lead with honesty and love, they get respect and love in return. Personal investment garners high reward.

*Rekindled? Yes!*

# Day 6
# THE FOCUS WAS CHRIST

## *Rx info-med*

In February 1982, I listened to a black man from Uganda tell the story of the East Africa Revival. He gave his talk at the Evangelical Bible Seminary of Southern Africa in Pietermaritzburg, South Africa. The message got through to me: I saw the power of God to handle anger.

The revival began in the late 1920s and early '30s when spiritual problems mounted so high that missionaries wanted to go home. Gospel workers felt depressed, angry, and burned out.

In 1935 two men, one black, the other white, were studying Scripture. They experienced a moment of genuine revelation. They learned, rather relearned, this grand and ancient truth: By the merits of the cross of Jesus, people can confess their sins and live victoriously over sin.

This illuminating discovery took revival dimensions. Whole nights of prayer, a spirit of oneness in Christ, multiplied conversions among Australians, Germans, and others in East Africa were accompanied by a remarkable variety of other miracles.

The hallmark of the revival was Jesus. He took central place—not miracles, not gifts of the Spirit, not other manifestations of His Presence, but Christ Himself. Jesus, missionaries and nationals learned together, is everything. In Him lies the secret. Focus on gifts and see jealousies emerge; zero in on healing and watch arguments surface; make manifestations central and observe hearts give birth to antagonisms. Interestingly, when the focus goes to anything but Christ, anger lifts its ugly head, producing a crop of hate.

The grand discovery, then, in the East Africa Revival is this: Jesus Christ occupies the primary place in individual lives, also in the group. It produces a crucial side effect—freedom from anger.

So how do we cooperate with God in making our Lord central?

**Putting and keeping Him there**—an act of the will.

**Making this act of the will a daily decision.** Expose yourself to influences that facilitate regular decisiveness: Bible meditation, devotional enlightenment, Christian conversation.

**Making the centralizing of Christ the pivot of your lifestyle.** Christ-centered style yields growth, which means holding steady in group discussion no matter how vigorous, remaining open to the deepening purification of the Spirit, and lovingly accepting all in fellowship with Christ.

*Rekindled? Yes!*

# Day 7 THE EAST AFRICA REVIVAL

## *Rx info-med*

The Jesus revival in East Africa had definite characteristics.

**Walking in the light.** Christians kept a clean conscience before God and one another. Pride, jealousy, and sins of thought and behavior came to confession. Hiding from one's offenses simply was not done. When one walked in darkness unwittingly, the Spirit turned light on the sins. Revealed, the moral violation came under intense internal censure, confession followed, then forgiveness.

The other day, coming out of my local U.S. Post Office, I met an overseas retreat leader back from Africa and talked with her a moment about the East Africa Revival. She picked up on it immediately and with a knowing smile commented, "Purity of conscience—yes, I witnessed it." The influence of the revival continues.

**Restitution.** Converted Christians returned stolen items. Shocked authorities listened to accounts of misbehavior. Grateful businessmen collected overdue debt money. In every case of restitution, miracles of transformation and good will took place.

**Brokenness.** Genuine humility issues in receiving criticism graciously. Preachers took corrections, Gospel workers submitted to admonitions, husbands and wives surrendered their differences and found reconciliation. In such a Spirit-oriented environment, hostilities simply did not have a chance to build up.

**The cross of Christ.** The biblical accounts of Jesus' finished work (1 Cor. 1:18; Eph. 2:16; Phil. 2:8) communicated with astonishing impact to all Spirit-filled Christians. The availability of the atonement for cleansing the human heart and sustaining that purity made its New Testament impression on sincere and receptive persons.

When this biblical Christianity invades a soul distraught by injustices and depressions, renewal sets in. Anyone experienced in vital Christianity knows the reality of erased resentments and the resulting sense of relief.

The radical and divine remedy for anger is awareness of sin, willing restitution, and resultant forgiveness. The radical remedy, then, goes a long way toward defining life in Christ.

***Rekindled? Yes!***

\*\*\*               \*\*\*               \*\*\*

## WEEK'S SUMMARY POINT OF
## HOPE AND HEALING

**Frozen anger often creates depression; forgiveness results in peace.**

# WEEK 13

# REKINDLED: DEALING WITH GUILT

He [the angel] touched my mouth with the coal and said,
"Look. This coal has touched your lips. Gone your guilt,
your sins wiped out."

—Isaiah 6:7, *The Message*


A man can stand a lot as long as he can stand himself.
He can live without hope, without books, without friends,
without music as long as he can listen to his own thoughts.

—Axel Munthe
*The Story of San Michele*


We come now to the third dragon, guilt. The first, fear, is the burden of the future; the second, anger, is the weight of the present;
the third, guilt, is the worry about the past.

# Day 1
## PERSPECTIVE

*Rx info-med*

Initially we need to remind ourselves of the difference
between guilt and guilt feelings. Real guilt centers in
wrongs actually done, objective sin. Guilt feelings may

or may not find their source in moral wrongdoing. Everyone does not have a conscience about violating God's laws; in contrast, some sense guilt when they have done nothing amiss. Conscientious persons can wrongly carry a load of guilt if they cannot go to every church meeting, help each person in need, and contribute to all worthy causes that come to their attention.

Elizabeth Kubler-Ross dedicated her life to relieving the fear and guilt of those in process of dying. She believed happy children in the Western world get contaminated as they grow and thus develop false guilt. A significant purpose of medicine, in her view, related to release from damaging guilt feelings.

All of us must sort out true from false guilt, from mere, unnecessary guilt feelings. Discover the New Testament teaching through an honest reading of the biblical text and God's grace to hear it.

**Honesty.** List your supposed wrongdoings. Eliminate what you only imagine as integrity breaks, testing uncertainties against Scripture. Bring obvious sins to God. Take as long as you need to assess your moral status but clear your conscience. The resulting peace makes the effort vastly worthwhile and can do wonders for those suffering burnout.

**Evaluation.** Arriving at a realistic perspective revolves around factors exaggerated or made complex by a scrupulous mind. A good spiritual director will ask an overly conscientious person, "Do you suffer from scruples?" Scruples cloud our minds. They inject hesitancies,

qualms, misgivings into our thinking. True, careless people do indeed need to examine their behavior with genuine care, but someone always questioning himself or herself suffers an unnecessary burden. Many a burnout victim lives with the strain of a scrupulous mind-set.

A young college professor, in charge of a small campus
activities account, spent money from the fund on a project, then had second thoughts. Did he misappropriate
funds? Wisely he spoke to his superior to clear the matter
and his conscience returned to rest. Get the kind of help
you need with ethically gray questions. Responsible
evaluation brings peace.

**God's grace.** Some wrongdoing cannot undergo correction because time and distance preclude clearing the air.
Only the rain of grace can create the fresh atmosphere
necessary for the soul to live and breathe freely. Sincere,
guileless Christians find God's grace operative in uncor-
rectable circumstances, like the death of a person you
have wronged but cannot put right even by talking to a
living relative.

*Rekindled? Yes!*

# Day 2

## JOYS OF A FREE MIND

### *Rx info-med*

The Axel Munthe quotation on the title page of this week's readings subtly reveals the joyous liberty of forgiven and released people. Feel yourself clear and clean, recovering from the fatigue of a bothersome conscience.

See Munthe's four illustrations—hope, books, friends, and music—as subjects of freedom for the mind uncluttered by nettling moral issues.

**Hope.** Hopeful persons exude optimism while guilty people give vent to pessimism. A Christian who cheated on his wife tried to cover his sin, arguing for the obsolescence of the *old* morality. Nothing worked happily—not his job, not his social relationships, not his plans for a better life. His total being took on dull, irritable, and burned-out coloration. Neither counseling nor medication put vibrancy back into his existence. When he finally faced his sin, confessed it to God and his wife, and experienced forgiveness, he lived comfortably with himself, his family, colleagues at work, and friends. Hope restored!

**Books.** Try to absorb yourself in a book when guilt courses down the runways of your mind! Perhaps escape reading will work for a little while, but sooner or later the culpability threat rears its ugly head. But the moral challenge faced and cleared frees the mind to relish an author's storyline, thus bringing needed diversion from the day's labor.

**Friends**. "You can't find anything better for beating fatigue," said an observer about a house party. Fun, food and fellowship have almost magical restorative powers. This medication does its fullest work for free persons, yet the one fighting guilt still needs restoration.

**Music**. Nothing captures one's soul like a Mozart symphony or a Vivaldi chamber work. Folk tunes possess power to express our feelings about the past, conjuring nostalgia. Music, whatever genre, whatever one's taste, is such a forceful healing tool that a whole therapeutic movement centers in it. One can earn a college degree in music therapy and land a job in a clinical center. How grand melodious sounds ring in the souls of forgiven and released persons!

Forgiven persons live in the emancipated environment of hope, books, friends, music, and the other God-given instruments of happiness.

***Rekindled? Yes!***

# Day 3

## CLEARING THE

## SUBCONSCIOUS MIND

### *Rx info-med*

A major factor in burnout is guilt hidden in the dark recesses of the subconscious mind. Vague hints surface now and again while undefined floating anxieties pester us. Some of the unconscious guilt comes from cultural sins like manipulation.

Manipulating people, robbing them of information, and slanting facts, renders us dishonest. In quiet moments we envision the ultimate implications and fear them. Beware! Because culture accepts and hides manipulation, we talk ourselves out of facing the moral facts and the way shuffling the cards can damage people.

We may not verbalize the thoughts but living with them is no picnic. They irritate because the radical nature of the Gospel invades our consciences as we read the New Testament. We need to halt the causes of our uneasy feelings.

*Invite the Holy Spirit to make you vividly aware of New Testament morality.* Little by little the Spirit reveals motivations that characterize our interpersonal relations. He gets specific about the way we conduct our money affairs, for example. Richard Foster helps us with his book, *The Challenge of the Disciplined Life: Money, Sex and Power* (1985, reprint 1999). Foster faces the issues, not only about money, while refusing to give an inch on Christian ethics and spirituality. We can become thoroughly alive to the freeing truth that will otherwise hurt us. The way we handle money, also sex and power, both for ourselves and others, may well be a moral development issue with which we must come to grips.

*Implement your emerging awareness.* Suppose I discover racial prejudice in myself. I had thought I enjoyed freedom from this sin; now I discover superiority feelings toward other peoples. I see my American ways above, for example, African ways or any other culture. I begin to read, gather information, and analyze my attitudes critically. The Spirit will inform me of specific ways I can put into action my dawning revelations.

Detecting guilt and doing something about it can be a major step to recovery from burnout. When one lives under the shadow of unresolved guilt, the inevitable result, sooner or later, is self-hatred. To the contrary when one faces up to guilt, confesses it, experiences forgiveness, resolution, renewal, and restoration, a wholesome self-image emerges.

**Rekindled? Yes!**

# Day 4

# GRAND BENEFITS OF A TIDY CONSCIENCE

### *Rx info-med*

John Woolman, eighteenth-century American Quaker, exercised forthright courageous conviction that made a difference. His belief in simplicity continues to challenge and influence the shape of our stewardship. His rugged personal honesty set in motion ripples of truth that spread over our culture. More, his quiet fight against slavery brought a halt among Friends to that despicable sin long before the Civil War. By 1770 no Quaker kept slaves.

Woolman had little going for him. He lived for only fifty-two years, never possessed the skill to organize a typical American protest movement, and lived with precious little physical strength, yet he achieved substantial goals.

**He refused to live with an untidy conscience.** To see a fellow human being in need was an occasion to meet that need, whatever the inconvenience. In his *Plea for the Poor*, he recommends work with the poverty-stricken to identify with their plight.

**He shaped his lifestyle to his calling.** This Quaker tailor cut off opportunities to develop his business for a number of reasons, one of the most important being to make possible the traveling ministry to which God called him. He lived on a meager income and determined nothing would hinder completion of his divine assignments. Deliberately refusing fame and fortune, he followed the Inner Light. He insisted on weaning himself from the world's image of greatness and disciplining his attitude toward money.

**He spoke strongly against evil.** His protests were not always verbal. As a guest at a farmhouse, he might quietly walk away from his noon meal to protest the host family keeping slaves. He was known to refuse writing a receipt for the sale of a black man. Though soft-spoken, he could offer probing questions to slave owners: What happens to you as a moral person when you keep slaves? What kind of justice education do you model for your children? For thirty years John Woolman rode his horse up and down the American East coast, pressing the claims of righteous living in his own calm, consistent, and persistent way.

Woolman listened to the Inner Voice. He developed a conscience sensitive to human need, thus making contagious a profoundly effective preventative medicine against guilt.

*Rekindled? Yes!*

# Day 5

# "CUMBERS"

### Rx info-med

John Woolman called encumbrances "cumbers" (Foster, *Freedom* 72-3). These burdens of guilt need unloading so heaviness does not create burnout. God calls us to give Him our cumbers: "… let us also lay aside every weight…" (Heb.12:1). Peterson renders this Scripture phrase, "Strip down, start running."

Take a look at a pair of cumbers.

**Using instead of building people.** Robert K. Greenleaf, in *Servant Leadership*, observes that some leaders see institutions as people developers. In that happy context persons grow into tall, healthy, strong, self-propelled workers. Other leaders use persons as devices to make the institution grow. Greenleaf rightly observes that the latter leaders succeed only for a time while the others endure.

Get rid of the people-using cumbers. They initiate burnout in employees, even in employers.

**Doing what looks good instead of what is good.** Be true to your best self. Unsullied labor as over against pretense achieves more in the long run than showing off.

Elton Trueblood describes an on-the-spot research about conversion. When twenty-five persons were asked how they met Christ, they indicated that an ordinary person served as the instrument. Not a conspicuous soul-winning personality or grand event did the business. God uses the humble servants to get His work done. True, God uses grand assemblies such as Billy Graham events to get His work done, but very often a quiet, unheralded person is His instrument. Content yourself with inconspicuous servanthood and watch the burden of *significance*, fraught with guilt overtones and burnout threat, fade away.

We all struggle with these temptations. Willingness to face deceptive attractions is a first step in unloading the guilt. Determining to rid oneself of such sin and guilt, then actually doing it is by forthright attack and repentance.

A Jewish legend says that when Satan was asked what he missed most about heaven, he replied, "the Trumpets in the morning." Burnout victims suffer low enthusiasm. Ridding ourselves of cumbers opens our soul's ear to the invigorating sound of new beginnings. When we hear trumpets in the morning, we know that God has moved redemptively to do something deep and profound about our guilt.

### *Rekindled? Yes!*

# Day 6

## HEALING FOR GUILT

### *Rx info-med*

Whether a sense of guilt results from objective wrongdoing or imaginary guilt accompanied by bad feelings, God provides healing and release. The following three medications speak to the conscience with remedial therapy.

**The sacraments heal.** Saints through the centuries commend, often in strong language, the sacraments as liberating treatment. The ancient and medieval Church thought of the Eucharist as medicine. No wonder pastors anoint for healing at services of Holy Communion. Forgiveness precedes healing; in conjunction with healing comes a new touch of God's Spirit. The Communion ritual calls for fresh forgiveness; the taking of the body and blood of our Lord is the infusion, newly experienced, of God's Spirit. Yes! In the Sacrament of Holy Communion, with confession and repentance, comes the washing away of guilt. *Sola gratia.*

The New Testament baptism-as-death-and-resurrection passage (early in Romans 6) tells us God graces us with surrender and resultant healing:

> When we are lowered into the water, it is like the burial of Jesus; when we are raised up out of the water, it is like the resurrection of Jesus. Each of us is raised into a light-filled world by our Father so that we can see where we're going in our new grace-sovereign country. Could it be any clearer?

Our old way of life was nailed to the Cross with Christ, a decisive end to that sin-miserable life–no longer at sin's every beck and call! What we believe is this: If we get included in Christ's sin-conquering death, we also get included in his life-saving resurrection. (MSG)

That figure of death and resurrection paints a clear picture of the guilt-free person. The renewal of that in-depth experience in covenant services reminds us of our liberation in Christ. *Sola gratia* again!

**The healing Word**  is also medicine. Martin Luther insisted that the spoken Word frees us—yes, but also sustains us. Nourishment and preservation come with the proclamation of Scripture. Luther said our souls can do without anything except God's Word, which provides truth, light, peace, righteousness, salvation, joy, and liberty. When we hear and receive the Gospel, we are fed, made righteous, set free, and rendered whole. Healthy Christians are healthy precisely because their guilts are exposed to God's Word spoken by the power of the Spirit, who releases the penitent searcher.

**Healing friends.** A Celtic proverb reminds us that, "Anyone without a soul friend is a body without a head."

Friendship is an *essential* of life. Living without friends compares to existing like a beast in the desert. Fellowship with spiritually knowing friends becomes a pathway, leading us closer to the love and knowledge of God. Someone observed that authentically Christian "friendship lies close to perfection."

Note this: One of our greatest deceptions is to believe we can free ourselves of burdens without the benefit of fellow travelers. But what therapy in a believing spouse! In a listening pastor! In a trusted prayer partner! Sharing opens the door to the Spirit's clarifying, forgiving, and healing ministries. Such therapy does great good to a person threatened by burnout!

A servant heart, given honorary degrees, asked in wonderment, "But why?" She simply could not understand the honors  and claimed only to be a listener to hurting people.  Well, that's quite enough. Quite enough.

### *Rekindled? Yes!*

# Day 7

## CONDONING OR FORGIVING?

*Rx info-med*

C. S. Lewis calls our attention to a fundamental and liberating truth about guilt:

> The demand that God should forgive ... [a man determined to do evil] while he remains what he is, is based on a confusion between condoning and forgiving. To condone an evil is simply to ignore it, to treat it as if it were good. But forgiveness needs to be accepted as well as offered if it is to be complete: and a man who admits no guilt can accept no forgiveness"( *Problem of Pain* 122 ).

While Freud taught the need to get rid of guilt—he saw it as a deterrent to health—he did not admit to the cause and effect relationship of sin and guilt. Yes, to get rid of the burden of wrongdoing is indeed enormously health-producing. The issue, however, relates to the authentic way of relieving the toxic feelings accompanying evil activity. Christians believe only God Himself, through repentance, can bring to reality that profound therapy. True, in-depth counseling may help straighten out the crooked lines in one's image of sin and its consequences, but divine grace defines the ultimate therapy.

Carl Menninger wrote a book called *Whatever Became of Sin?* A good question! Human beings have all sorts of ways to persuade themselves that sinful behavior is not really breaking the Law of God. Some deny the authenticity of the Law—*it is a concept that grew up in the so-*

*cial evolution of the race but has no permanent or uni-versal reality.* Some say, "Everyone does it," *so how can it be wrong?* Some believe that if they do a particular sin over and over they will become *numb to it and thus erase its ill effects from their conscience.* Still others blame *childhood conditioning and thus exonerate themselves.*

Yes, such perspectives hold some truth, and we do well to take those factors seriously. But analysis, however factual, possesses only limited therapeutic power.

While we have all sorts of ways of excusing ourselves, none of these, however clever or creative, can free the human spirit. To deny the *moral ought* God put inside normal men and women will only prove we cannot live against the Almighty without suffering serious consequences. How many burnout victims are heavy with such misperceptions!

To the contrary, living in cooperation with the revealed Word of God, and the God in us, results in enormous energy. That energy, ever value-oriented, means creativity instead of bland existence, possibilities instead of paralysis, love instead of fear, integration instead of splintering, worship instead of self-preoccupation, joy instead of sadness.

**Rekindled? Yes!**

\*\*\*                    \*\*\*                    \*\*\*

## WEEK'S SUMMARY POINT OF
## HOPE AND HEALING

**Jesus welcomes His family members to the fellowship of the forgiven.**

# SELECT BIBLIOGRAPHY

This bibliography will not only indicate source material, but also enrich the reader's knowledge. For example, James Martin's book provides up-to-date information on humor, and Laura Landro's *Wall Street Journal* piece gives fresh insight into how doctors can maintain emotional stability while treating patients with compassion.

à Kempis, Thomas. *Imitation of Christ*. Put into contemporary English by Donald E. Demaray. Stanton Island: Alba, 1997. Print.

Allen, David E., Lewis P. Bird, and Robert Herrmann, eds. *Whole Person Medicine: An International Symposium*. Downers Grove: InterVarsity, 1980. Print.

"America Shapes Up." *Time* 2 Nov. 1981: 106-15. Print.

Aquinas, Thomas. *My Way of Life: The Summa Simplified for Everyone*. Ed. Walter Farrell and Martin J. Healy. Brooklyn: Confraternity of the Precious Blood, 1952. Print.

Badham, Leslie. *Verdict on Jesus*. London: Hodder and Stoughton, 1971. Print.

Bastian, Donald N. *God's House Rules: Seven Biblical Truths to Transform and Enrich Your Family Life*. Toronto: BPS, 2007. Print.

Barzun, Jacques, ed. *Pleasures of Music: An Anthology about Music and Musicians*. London: U of Chicago Press, 1977. Print.

Beasley-Topliffe, Keith, ed. *The Upper Room Dictionary of Christian Spiritual Formation.* Nashville: Upper Room, 2003. Print.

Begley, Sharon. "Stress." *Saturday Evening Post* Nov/Dec 2011: 36-39. Print.

Billings, J. Todd. "How to Read the Bible." *Christianity Today* Oct. 2011: 28. Print.

Bombeck, Erma. *Aunt Erma's Cope Book.* New York: Fawcett, 1981. Print.

*Brain Rules by John Medina.* Pear Press, 2012. Web. 3 July 2012.

Brey, Robin L. "The Adolescent Brain: What Neurology Can Teach Us about Protecting Teens." *Neurology Now* Dec. 2011/Jan. 2012: 9. Print.

Bruce, F. F. *The New Testament Documents: Are They Reliable?* Downers Grove, IL: IVP, 1981. Rpt. of *Are the New Testament Documents Reliable?* 1943. Print.

Burpo, Todd, with Lynn Vincent. *Heaven Is for Real: A Little Boy's Astounding Story of His Trip to Heaven and Back.* Nashville: Thomas Nelson, 2010. Print.

Cowman, L. B. *Streams in the Desert: 366 Daily Devotional Readings.* Ed. Jim Reimann. Grand Rapids: Zondervan, 1997. Print.

Cousins, Norman. *Anatomy of an Illness as Perceived by the Patient.* New York: W. W. Norton and Co., 1979. Print.

Crab, Larry, Jr. "Moving the Couch into the Church." *Christianity Today* 22 Sept. 1978: 17-19. Print.

Demaray, Donald E., and Kenneth W. Pickerill. *A Robust Ministry: Keeping a Pure Heart, Clear Head, and*

*Steady Hand*. Nappanee, IN: Evangel Publishing House, 2004. Print.

Donaldson, Doug. "The Giggle Cure: Science Has Long Believed Laughter Is Good Medicine. Now There's Proof." *The Saturday Evening Post* May/June 2011: 25-29. Print.

Drucker, Peter F. "Know Thy Time." *Leadership* Spring 1982: 38-48. Print.

Eagleman, David. *The Secret Lives of the Brain*. New York: Pantheon, 2011. Print.

Eastman, Max, and William F. Fry. *The Enjoyment of Laughter*. New Brunswick: Transaction, 2009. Print.

"East-West Church & Ministry Report." 12.2 Wilmore: Asbury U, Spring 2004. Print journal.

"11% of Americans Taking Antidepressants." *Lexington Herald-Leader* 20 Oct. 2011: C10. Print.

Engstrom, Ted W., and Edward R. Dayton. "Time for Things That Matter." *Leadership,* Spring 1982: 16-29. Print.

Engstrom, Ted W., and David J. Juroe. *The Work Trap*. Old Tappan: Revell, 1979. Print.

"Exercise and Depression." *Harvard Health Publications*, Harvard Medical School. http://www.health.harvard.edu.

Foster, Richard J. *Celebration of Discipline: The Path to Spiritual Growth*. Rev. ed. San Francisco: Harper, 1988. Print.

Foster, Richard J., and James Bryan Smith. *Devotional Classics: Selected Readings for Individuals & Groups*. San Francisco: Harper San Francisco, 1993. Print.

Foster, Richard J. *Freedom of Simplicity.* San Francisco: Harper & Row, 1981.

---. *Money, Sex and Power: The Challenge of the Disciplined Life.* San Francisco: Harper, 1987. Reprinted as *The Challenge of the Disciplined Life: Reflections on Money, Sex, and Power.* Hodder and Stoughton, 1999. Print.

---. *Prayer: Finding the Heart's True Home.* Harper San Francisco, 1992. Print.

---. *Sanctuary of the Soul: Journey into Meditative Prayer.* Downers Grove, IL: IVP Books, 2011. Print.

Foster, Richard J., and Emile Griffin. *Spiritual Classics: Selected Readings for Individuals and Groups on the Twelve Spiritual Disciplines.* San Francisco: Harper, 2000.

Freudenberger, Herbert J. with Geraldine Richelson. *Burn-Out: The High Cost of High Achievement.* Garden City: Anchor Press, 1980. Print.

Gardner, John W. *Self-Renewal: The Individual and the Innovative Society.* New York: Harper and Row, 1963. Print.

Goleman, Daniel. *Emotional Intelligence:* Why *It Can Matter More than IQ.* New York: Bantam Books, 1995. Print.

Gray, Sandra C. "The Message of Easter: I Am the One Jesus Loves." Asbury University, Wilmore. April 2011. Address.

Greenleaf, Robert K. *Servant Leadership.* New York: Paulist, 1977. Print.

Gross, Martin L. "Conversation with an Author: Erma Bombeck." [interview] *Book Digest* 9 Sept. 1978. Print.

Hammarskjold, Dag. *Markings.* Trans. Leif Sjoberg and W. H. Auden. London: Faber and Faber, 1966. Print.

"Headache Sufferers: Help is on the Way." *U. S. News and World Report* 24 May 1982: 74-75. Print.

Hoffman, Edward. "This Way to Memory Lane." *Guideposts* Jan. 2012: 24-33. Print.

Hosking, Julia. "Compassion Fatigue: Is Ministry Leaving You Tired, Numb or Overwhelmed? You're Not Alone." *Salvationist* Aug. 2011: 16. Print.

Houghton, Frank. *Amy Carmichael of Dohnavur: The Story of a Lover and Her Beloved.* Fort Washington: Christian Literature Crusade, n.d. Print.

Jones, E. Stanley. *Abundant Living*. Nashville: Abingdon Festival, 1976. Print.

---. *Christian Maturity*. Nashville: Abingdon Festival, 1980. Print.

---. *Growing Spiritually*. Nashville: Abingdon Festival, 1978. Print.

---. *A Song of Ascents: A Spiritual Autobiography.* Nashville: Abingdon, 1968. Print.

---. *The Word Become Flesh.* Rev. ed. Nashville: Abingdon, 2006. Print.

Kehl, D. B. "Burnout: The Risk of Reaching Too High." *Christianity Today* 20 Nov. 1981: 26-28. Print.

Landro, Laura. "Poetry, Painting to Earn an M.D." *The Wall Street Journal* 1 Feb. 2011: D1. Print.

Larson, Bruce. *There's a Lot More to Health than Not Being Sick.* Waco: Word, 1981. Print.

Laubach, Frank C. *Letters of a Modern Mystic.* Westwood: Revell, 1958. Print.

Leacock, Stephen. "My Financial Career." *Literary Lapses*, 1910. *The Library*. The Virtual Community, 18 Dec. 2005. Web. 3 July 2012.

Lewis, C. S. *A Grief Observed.* London: Faber & Faber, 1961 edition published under the pseudonym N. W. Clerk; reissued 1963 under C. S. Lewis. Print.

---. *The Problem of Pain.* N. Y.: The Macmillan Company, 1962. Print.

Lonsdale, David. "Examen." *The Upper Room Dictionary of Christian Spiritual Formation.* Nashville: Upper Room, 2003. 99-100. Print.

Martin, James. *Between Heaven and Mirth: Why Joy, Humor and Laughter Are at the Heart of the Spiritual Life.* New York: HarperOne, 2011. Print.

Maslach, Christian, Susan E. Jackson, Michael P. Leiter, Wilmar B. Schaufeli, and Richard L. Schwab. "Maslach Burnout Inventory (MBI)." *Mindgarden.com.* Mind Garden, Feb. 2012. Web. 3 July 2012.

Medina, John. *Brain Rules: 12 Principles for Surviving and Thriving at Work, Home and School.* Seattle: Pear, 2008. Print.

Menninger, Carl. *Whatever Became of Sin?* New York: Bantam, 1988. Print.

Menninger, Karl, with Jeanette Lyle Menninger. *Love Against Hate.* New York: Harvest-Harcourt, 1970. Print.

Merton, Thomas. *Seven Storey Mountain.* New York: Harcourt, 1948. Print.

Messner, Robert. "Burnout: Its Relevance to the Christian Physician." *Christian Medical Society Journal* Jan. 1982: 11-14. Print.

Miller, Tom. "Depression in Women." *Health and Wellness* May 2011: 12. Print.

Moll, Bob. "We Are Family." *Books and Culture* Nov./Dec. 2011: 19. Print.

Morley, Robert. *Book of Worries.* New York: Macmillan, 1980. Print.

"Nutritional Psychosis." *Omni* 4.8 Oct. '81: 45-46. Print.

Oden, Thomas C. *Classical Christianity: A Systematic Theology.* New York: Harper One, 2009. Print.

Paturel, Amy. "Buzz Kill: How Does Alcohol Affect the Teenage Brain?" *Neurology Now* Dec. 2011/Jan. 2012: 23-28. Print.

Peale, Norman Vincent. *Dynamic Imaging: The Powerful Way to Change Your Life.* Old Tappan: Revell, 1982. Print.

---. *Stay Alive All Your Life.* New York: Fawcett, 1978 . Print.

Peterson, Eugene H. "Interview." *Response* Autumn 2011: 18. Print.

---. *The Pastor: A Memoir.* New York: Harper One, 2011. Print.

Potter, Beverly. *Beating Job Burnout.* New York: Ace, 1980. Print.

"Protect Yourself from Alzheimer's Disease." *Reader's Digest* Dec. 2011/Jan. 2012:39-40. Print.

"Remembrance." *Dictionary of Biblical Imagery.* Downers Grove: InterVarsity, 1998. 702-03. Print.

Reynolds, Gretchen. "Exercise as the Foundation of Youth: Athletes Retain Muscle Mass, Study Shows." *Lexington Herald-Leader* 10 Nov. 2011: B12. Print.

Riggar, T. F. *Stress and Burnout: An Annotated Bibliog-raphy.* Carbondale: Southern Illinois Univeristy Press, 1985. Print.

Rivadeneira, Caryn. "The Science of Shaking Up: Why Cohabitating Couples are Putting Their Future at Risk." *Christianity Today* Sept. 2011: 69. Print.

"Salt: A New Villain?" *Time* 15 Mar. 1982: 64-71. Print.

Sebastian, Charles. "Anxiety Attacks." *Health and Well-ness* Nov. 2011: 17+. Print

Selye, Hans. *The Stress of Life.* Rev. ed. New York: McGraw, 1976. Print.

---. *Stress without Distress.* Philadelphia: Lippincott, 1974. Print.

Shanton, Steve. "Attitude Determines Altitude: ALS Can't Take Away My Father's Spirit." *Neurology Now* Oct./Nov. 2011: 80. Print.

Shedd, Charlie W. *Time for All Things: Meditations on the Christian Management of Time.* Nashville: Ab-ingdon-Apex, 1972. Print.

Small, Gary, with Gigi Vorgan. *The Alzheimer's Preven-tion Program: Keep Your Brian Healthy for the Rest of Your Life.* New York: Workman, 2011. Print.

Sparks, Martha. "Martha's Caregiver Journal: It's True, Laughter is Good Medicine." *Health and Wellness* May 2011: 14. Print.

Stevenson, Harry. "The Cross Straightened Me Out." *By His Stripes: 2011 Devotional Guide.* Wilmore: Free Methodist Church. 43. Print.

Teresa, Mother of Calcutta. *A Gift for God.* New York: Harper, 1975. Print.

"Time for All Things That Matter: A Conversation with Ted Engstrom and Ed Dayton." *Leadership* Spring 1982: 16-29. Print.

Tournier, Paul. *Secrets*. Trans. Joe Embry Richmond: Knox, 1965. Print.

Trobisch, Walter. *I Married You.* New York: Harper, 1975. Print.

Trueblood, Elton. *The Humor of Christ.* New York: Harper, 1964. Print.

VERSE and VOICE daily scripture and compelling quotes, July 20, 2011. Sojourners: Sojo-Mail@sojo.net.

Woolman, John, *The Journal and Major Essays* edited by Phillips P. Moulton. NY: Oxford University Press, 1971.

Wright, N. T. *Surprised by Hope: Rethinking Heaven, the Resurrection, and the Mission of the Church.* New York: HarperOne, 2009. Print.

Wulf, Andrea. *Founding Gardeners: Shaping of the American Nation.* New York: Kopf, 2011. Print.

CPSIA information can be obtained at www.ICGtesting.com
Printed in the USA
LVOW132043040613

336947LV00002BA/544/P